MW01107174

Absolutely Al

Absolutely Al

How Al Gray Dealt With Mobsters, Mental
Illness, Marital Woes and the KGB

Gary Stromberg

iUniverse, Inc.
New York   Bloomington

Absolutely Al
How Al Gray Dealt With Mobsters,
Mental Illness, Marital Woes and the KGB

Copyright © 2010 Gary Stromberg

All rights reserved. No part of this book may be used or reproduced by any means, graphic, electronic, or mechanical, including photocopying, recording, taping or by any information storage retrieval system without the written permission of the publisher except in the case of brief quotations embodied in critical articles and reviews.

iUniverse books may be ordered through booksellers or by contacting:

iUniverse
1663 Liberty Drive
Bloomington, IN 47403
www.iuniverse.com
1-800-Authors (1-800-288-4677)

Because of the dynamic nature of the Internet, any Web addresses or links contained in this book may have changed since publication and may no longer be valid. The views expressed in this work are solely those of the author and do not necessarily reflect the views of the publisher, and the publisher hereby disclaims any responsibility for them.

ISBN: 978-1-4502-2923-4 (sc)
ISBN: 978-1-4502-2924-1 (dj)
ISBN: 978-1-4502-2925-8 (ebk)

Printed in the United States of America

iUniverse rev. date: 05/25/2010

Dedication from Al Gray

This book is dedicated in loving memory of my parents Rob and Lottie Gray, and my beloved older brother Louis.

Special dedications to my two wonderful children Lottie and Rachel, and their mother Anita Gray.

And to my grandchild Azzizi Shalom Gray and other grandchildren that may follow.

To my sister-in-law Ruth Gray, my niece Carol Gray Marger, her husband Bill, and their three children Eli, Meg and Bernie.

To all of the great people in this book who provided the special commentary on the circumstances of my life.

And finally to Gary Stromberg and his wife Patty, who have been such good friends in bringing this book to fruition.

……..Al Gray

Contents

Preface

The telephone rings in the office of a movie producer in Hollywood. The producer picks up the phone, and is greeted by a well-known scriptwriter.

"Hello, Phil. I want to pitch a script to you."

"What do you have, Steve?"

"Well it's a story about a guy who travels to England with his family. The trip goes very po orly, and they decide to come back home a couple of days early. They get home, and two days later, they find out the flight they were supposed to be on, is blown up by terrorists."

"Go on."

"Well the guy takes this trip to the Soviet Union. The CIA asks him to take some photographs over there, and he gets nabbed by the KGB. And on another trip, the same guy and his wife are cornered at some airport in Russia. The KGB strip-searches both of them because they are convinced they are trying to smuggle a document."

"Okay, what else?"

"Well, this same guy is worried about his father, because he is in pretty deep with some bad guys over some big-time gambling debts. All of a sudden, the father just vanishes and is never heard from again."

"Then what happens?"

"The son has a tough time with all of this, and eventually develops mental problems. He starts stockpiling guns and a couple of times, he holds his wife hostage. One night, he is carted off to jail after he fired a gun during a confrontation with his wife."

"Okay, I follow you."

"So, then the guy winds up in a psychiatric hospital, and is determined to get things straightened out."

"Is he able to get back on track?"

"Well the guy puts his life together, he resumes his life as a wizard in the stock market, and becomes a big philanthropist."

"Okay Steve, thanks for the call. All of that sounds interesting enough, but to tell you the truth, it's too far-fetched. No one will ever believe it."

An Overwhelming Close Call

The London restaurant was nothing fancy. Pedestrian at best. A casual place for an American family to grab a casual dinner. Al and Anita Gray were visiting London along with their two young daughters. Lottie was nine, and Rachel, seven. Al says the restaurant reminded him of one of those Kenny King's restaurants back in Cleveland. Affordable. Comfortable.

The family sat down at a table, and Anita put her purse on a chair at an adjoining table. It was just an arms-length away. Anita was forty years old. Al was considerably older. In a few months he would be marking his sixty-first birthday.

The family had arrived in London a couple of days earlier. Al wanted to attend a meeting of World ORT. The Organization for Rehabilitation through Training. He was on the board, and thought it was important he attend this quarterly meeting.

ORT was founded some 100 years earlier in Czarist Russia. Its goal is to assist young people pursue technical subjects such as engineering and physics. Al devoted much of his time to Jewish organizations like ORT.

Catching a Pan Am flight out of New York to travel to this meeting shouldn't have been a big deal for Al. But it was. Mental illness was beginning to take hold of Al's life.

"I was not in good shape. I was upset I was going to have to take this type of trip in a short period of time. The meetings were only a day and a half. I decided I couldn't make this trip without Anita and the girls."

Al needed the support of his family. Perhaps spending a few days with them in London after the ORT meeting wrapped up, would ease the tensions in his life.

They looked over the menus in that London restaurant that Saturday evening. The plan was to fly Wednesday evening from Heathrow to J.F.K. in New York. They would change planes for the last leg of the trip to Cleveland.

It is difficult to remember if the food was good that night. The meal itself was quickly forgotten. A more important matter surfaced when the family got up and was about to leave the restaurant.

Anita said, "We had a table for four in a corner. I placed my purse between me and Rachel. At the table right across from us, there was a sandy-haired British kid. He sat down alone and I saw him slouching. I didn't pay much attention. I saw him smiling and he looked me in the eyes. He left, and when we got up to leave, I said, 'Where's my purse?'"

The table where the Gray family was seated was in the basement of the restaurant. Anita had noticed that the young man who sat at the next table, was carrying an umbrella. He apparently used the handle of that umbrella to snag the purse.

Al said, "I felt about as crappy as you could feel."

And why not? Anita's purse held not only cash, but the airline tickets for the return trip, as well as all four passports.

Al said, "She was not one to be sloppy about her belongings and felt a little guilty."

Al, Anita and the girls could do little to rectify the situation on Sunday. Monday morning, they headed to the American Embassy to get temporary passports. They went to the Pan Am ticket office in London to get their airplane tickets reissued.

"We considered getting the heck out of there. It wasn't a bad idea. To wait until Wednesday, feeling not so good, the purse being stolen, created pressure. I thought it was a good idea to just leave Monday evening."

The members of the Gray family took off that night from Heathrow. Their trip to London had been disrupted and truncated. As the plane reached cruising altitude, Al and Anita no doubt felt a bit of regret that their trip was ruined by a heartless thief. Those concerns were soon to fade.

Al and Anita awoke that Thursday morning back home in Cleveland. They turned on their television, and like most Americans, struggled to decipher what those people in Lockerbie, Scotland were talking about. It soon sunk in. Pan Am 103, a transatlantic flight that had departed Heathrow Wednesday evening, had blown up in mid-air. That was the flight Al, Anita, Lottie and Rachel were originally scheduled to take. Their plans were changed because of the stolen purse.

Al said, "That was quite a jolt to realize the flight we had been scheduled on had blown up."

Al was able to put it all together in about twenty seconds. The theft of Anita's purse, a twist of fate, had saved their lives.

Lottie said, "For me, it makes me appreciate what is, instead of what could have been. I have told the story many times, and to me, that's a significant event in my life because things could have been very different."

Al said, "I felt like the luckiest guy in the world. We both thought it was awful all those people died. We were glad we were not on it. We were glad our kids were not on it. I think it caused me to be appreciative of what I call the luck of the draw."

It was December 21, 1988 when that ill-fated Pan Am 747 lifted off. Flight 103 was the third Pan Am flight of the day to J.F.K. This aircraft carried the name Clipper Maid of the Sea. Two-hundred-forty-three passengers died that night. Sixteen crew members also perished. One-hundred-ninety of the dead were Americans. Four members of the Gray family could have made that total 194.

Rachel said, "I have a memory of the plane crash, but at the time I was too young to realize that we were supposed to be on that flight. I was only seven, so I didn't learn the complete story until I was older."

Al said, "The tragedy wouldn't keep me from getting on an airplane. The bombing could discourage one from wanting to travel on an airplane. It really didn't for me. In a car, the odds are more likely you will be hurt or killed than on an airplane. Worry just isn't a way you can lead your life. Of course you don't want to die too soon and leave things undone. If the purse hadn't been stolen, we would have died."

Rachel said, "As long as the four of us are alive, it will always be in the back of our minds. It's part of our story."

The Disappearance

Al was grateful that a twist of fate in London saved his life, but just getting through a day was becoming more and more of a challenge. He was sixty years old. That was the exact age of Al's father Rob when he walked out of the family's Cleveland Heights apartment and was never seen again. Al was haunted by his father's disappearance.

Al maintains he fell victim to anniversary syndrome. He plunged into the depths of mental illness when he turned sixty. Reaching that age somehow triggered an explosion of uncontrollable emotions. His dad's life apparently ended at sixty. Now Al's life was spiraling out of control. He did his best to press on. "I think I did relatively well considering what the illness was doing to me daily. I was buffeted around by it. I had a great deal of problems. I sought the aid of a couple of doctors who couldn't figure it out. I wasn't getting adequate treatment for it. Whatever meds I was taking, didn't work. The drugs had not been refined back then. The doctors I went to were good, but their treatment was not effective."

Rob Gray ran a moving company that moved mainly Jewish residents of Cleveland's Glenville neighborhood into new homes in Cleveland

Heights. He worked hard every day. He was usually chomping on a cigar. At night, he would take it easy, leafing through the afternoon newspaper. He had a great sense of humor. He knew how to craft a joke with the best of them. He was bald. He had a large belly.

Al says Rob Gray was a great father. Al's only sibling was his brother Louis, who was ten years older. The family moved around, living in apartments and rental houses. His father never owned a home. It sometimes got rough, especially during the Great Depression. But Al says his family was never evicted.

Rob Gray had a major vice. He loved to gamble. It was a burden on his family. Times were tough enough. A thin budget was stretched even thinner. He would go to a gambling club on Harvard Avenue and play cards. He gambled his money away.

"I thought of him in relation to my mother, and the hurt and anger that came out of it. She would say, 'Rob, you are killing us. You are making our lives intolerable.' She was a kindly, sweet woman. She was lovely."

The marriage of Lottie and Robert Gray was strained. Divorce was not common in those days. Al wondered, however, how much longer the marriage might last. Gambling became a huge issue.

"Like all habits, if they can't be controlled, you are in big trouble."

During the years Al attended Cleveland Heights High, his family rented a house on Silsby, not far from Lee. The rent was fifty-two dollars a month during those war years. At the end of the war, the family moved into an apartment building on Mayfield. It was near Hampshire Lane.

On December 7, 1952, Rob Gray stepped out of the apartment and headed to the garage where his car was parked. Al surmised he went out there to smoke a cigar. The following morning, he saw footprints in the snow leading to the car. The car never moved. There was no trace of Al's father.

Al was twenty-four. He had completed law school. Did his father flee the area to get away from gangsters he owed money? Or did those mobsters take Rob to a remote area and kill him because of his failure to settle up on gambling debts?

Al's sister-in-law, Ruth Gray, remembers, "There was going to be a wedding in the family. Rob's younger brother Hy was getting married. Rob disappeared just before the wedding. Al's father was involved in gambling. My husband Louis was working downtown at a drugstore, and just before the disappearance, he was told by somebody they were looking for his father."

Al wrote letters to police in Los Angeles, Chicago, Detroit and Pittsburgh. He figured his dad may have taken off to a large city since he had never lived in a small town. He knew his dad had no money. He couldn't imagine that Rob would abandon his mother, only to settle in some other part of Cleveland.

Al said, "His disappearance overwhelmed her. She tried not to show it. Soon after he left, I took to her see a movie at the Cedar-Lee. It had a romantic theme and I noticed that she started crying."

Al knew his mother still loved her husband, but he says that love had been dampened over the years by all of the gambling problems.

"She didn't complain a lot, she was not a complaining person. She felt horrendous about what happened."

Al's good friend Alan Schonberg spoke glowingly of Al's mother.

"His mother was a saint. I have never known a woman I could think more highly of than his mother. He honored his mother as much as a son could honor his mother. She was pure sweetness and love. A pretty woman. A beautiful woman. She was gracious, smart and giving. I have fond memories of her."

The disappearance of Rob Gray stunned the entire, close-knit Gray family in Cleveland. Al's cousin Rita Gray Newman recalls how shocked family members were.

"The family really didn't talk about it. It was traumatic. We knew it happened. We just didn't talk about it."

Lottie Gray had gone into the work force the year before her husband disappeared. She worked at the Auto Club. It was housed in an old mansion on Euclid Avenue. The site eventually became part of the campus of Cleveland State University. Lottie was a bookkeeper in the Auto Club membership department. She stayed with that job until she retired decades later.

The mystery of his dad's disappearance haunted Al. He wrote to newspapers. He sent out photographs. Police officers said they had never seen Rob Gray. Al feared that his father ran off because he grew tired of listening to Al chastise him for gambling all the time. Was he living out his life in Idaho?

Al's psychiatrist worked with him, urging him to stop blaming himself.

Al said, "Now, I think the gamblers killed him and threw his body in a river. Early on, my mental struggles centered on the fact I couldn't accept that he was probably killed by gamblers. I didn't think it had happened. It may have been an obvious conclusion that they killed him, but it didn't occur to me."

Whenever Al confronted his father about playing cards and losing all of his money, his dad had tried to reassure him that he was doing the best he could to keep things together. Al was an emotional wreck. He had been very close to his father. His father was proud of Al's accomplishments.

Alan Schonberg said, "Al was a respectful son."

Al was disappointed that his father was consumed with gambling, but he doesn't want to diminish the influence his father had on him.

"I learned an enormous amount from my dad, and I shouldn't knock him. My dad was a great guy. He raised me to be honest. He raised me to be bright. He raised me to work hard and to get ahead in the world. A lot of my charitable instincts come out of him. He had very healthy instincts about helping people, not only financially, but emotionally as well. He would help people get opportunities in life."

In the years after his dad vanished, Al pressed on with his work as a young lawyer. As time went on, however, there was a gradual decline in his mental stability.

He had dated Anita for six years and finally married her in 1975 when he was forty-seven. As his outlook deteriorated, the marriage began to unravel. Al, perhaps in an attempt to empower himself, started buying guns. He got most of them at Atlantic Gun and Tackle on Northfield. He went to shooting ranges to learn how to operate them.

In 1990, Al and Anita traveled to New York City. A gala banquet was to be held at the Waldorf-Astoria to commemorate the fiftieth anniversary of the United Jewish Appeal. Anita had been very active with the organization, and when she failed to appear at the banquet, there was a great deal of concern.

Anita said, "Al was just really ill and he had a breakdown. He refused to let me out of the hotel room to go to the banquet. My fear at that point was he was going to jump out of the window at the Waldorf. I thought he was going to commit suicide, so I didn't want to leave. When I didn't show up at the banquet, they sent people upstairs. He wouldn't let me leave, and wouldn't let me open the door. So then it became very public. The police were involved. That lasted several hours."

When they returned to Cleveland, Anita insisted that Al get psychiatric help. The psychiatrist informed her that Al was stockpiling guns.

"I was so shocked. This sweet, gentle man. It was so bizarre. I had little kids in the house, so it was hard to deal with. His behavior was due to his illness. I never asked him why he was doing these things. He was paranoid and manic depressive. Manic depressive, you can deal with. Paranoia, you can't. You can't reason with someone who is paranoid. It's a total waste of time to try. It's very scary."

Anita realized Al's mental state was getting worse, but she tried to live every day as normally as she could.

"It was really intense and painful. It was difficult to see this great fall from grace."

She said the illness would manifest itself at night. She chose to move out of the bedroom of their home. The stockpiling of weapons was a signal that time was running out on the marriage.

"One morning he held me hostage with a gun for four hours. My concern was getting the kids out. I said just let the kids go to school. Get them dressed. I stayed in the house and he took them out to meet the bus. He came back into the house. I figured the best thing for me to do is wait. It was pretty brutal, but I waited it out."

She insisted he check himself into the psychiatric unit at Mt. Sinai. She told Al if he didn't, she was going to leave him. He realized he had his back to the wall.

Al's mental setbacks were having an obvious impact on his ability to work.

His law partner Bob Luria said, "It was very hard. A couple of times, we transported him to a facility. He had anxiety attacks at work. He was in a dark place."

Al's other law partner Keith Belkin said, "Early on, there were things we should have picked up on. Things that were different. He was a little erratic. Bob and I knew there were some problems. We had some discussions with him. He just never did anything about it until things got so bad, something had to be done about it."

The third major incident was by far the most frightening. The children were in bed. The family lived on Parkland Drive in Shaker Heights.

Anita said, "I knew he had a gun in his pocket. I knew these incidents had gotten progressively worse. I made a calculated decision to leave the house. We were in the kitchen and it took me three hours to move from the kitchen table to see if the door was open or not. I just ran out of the house. I'm running down the driveway and I heard the gun fire. I don't believe he fired at me. I think he just fired into the air. That ended everything."

He was attempting to frighten Anita. She declined to call the police, but a concerned neighbor did. Al Gray was taken off to jail.

On occasion, Al would serve as a lawyer for people who had been arrested. He would appear in Shaker Heights Municipal Court, and was known to most of the attorneys there. So the morning after his arrest, when he was ushered into court wearing a white jail jumpsuit, his acquaintances there were taken aback. They were startled to see him as a defendant.

Anita said, "The police wanted to have attempted murder charges filed. I refused to cooperate. I said he's not a murderer. He's sick."

Anita didn't want Al sent to prison, but she knew this was the last episode.

"His psychiatrist said to me, 'You've got to get a divorce, or this man will kill you.'"

Al was released on bond and was admitted to the Laurelwood Psychiatric Hospital in Willoughby. It would be his home for the next five months.

Al said, "I felt humiliated to be there, but I was relieved I no longer had any guns. They were dangerous for me. I surrendered them to my psychiatrist. Laurelwood was fabulous."

Anita thought it was vital he get intense care.

"He was like a walking time-bomb. We are very lucky it didn't turn into a major tragedy."

Al Gray's mental woes had been brewing for some time. Few realized what was happening.

Al said, "I experienced a fair amount of mental issues before my mental illness became paramount. My issues with my father's disappearance were part of my life the whole time, and not just during the time of my mental illness. It was an ongoing challenge I had not dealt with honestly and completely."

Al's cousin, Anita Gray Newman, was living in Dallas when Al's mental issues worsened.

She said, "The worst part was not knowing what to do. How do you reach out to someone who is going through that, and not knowing really what that person is actually going through."

Al's previous stays in the psychiatric unit at Mt. Sinai Hospital both lasted less than a month and were not helpful to his mental woes.

"Anita would bring the girls to visit me at Laurelwood four times a week. I would say their visits saved my life. At least, they ensured my recovery."

Rachel said, "I do remember being at Laurelwood, being uncomfortable around some of the patients because they were obviously mentally ill in their behavior. I don't remember my dad ever acting like that. There were some really mentally ill people there who were low-functioning, maybe having medication adjustments, who behaviorally weren't as normal as others. I wasn't frightened, just uncomfortable."

Lottie said, "I remember a lot about being there. I remember the other patients and how gracious the staff was. Children were not allowed in the unit, but they would let us come in and go to the cafeteria, eat, and play basketball in the gym. I was in middle school. I didn't know how to explain to my friends about going there so often, because nobody knew what mental illness was at my age. So there was a lot of emotion going on. Dad really appreciated the visits. We would sometimes meet in the conference room. I remember we lit Hanukah candles with dad and Howard. He was one of the patients who was Jewish. Howard really appreciated being with us."

Anita tried her best to explain what was going on to Lottie and Rachel. She told them the mind can get sick, just like a stomach or a leg can get sick.

Al's friend Jordan Rothkopf said, "I recall going to Laurelwood to visit him and it was emotional for me, because here was a commanding man I knew. To see him at a psychiatric hospital was tough. I can still see the room in my mind. It had a major effect on me."

Earlier in his life, Al had done his best to control the growing rage brewing inside him.

"I overdid self-control. One of the challenges in my law practice was to be able to control my temper so I could deal with situations that could overwhelm me as a lawyer. I tried to do better in the courtroom and in the judge's chamber than the other guy."

Al thinks a flare-up of anger can easily become an explosion of anger.

"I think a lot of anger is false. You have to resist false anger. You have to learn to control it and convert it into a positive for self-discipline. I am an enormous believer in self-discipline. There can be a point at which you just convince yourself to be angry. If you should get a minor amount of anger over a situation, and you don't restrain yourself, it could falsely become excessive to the point that it hurts you to be angry."

Controlling his anger over everyday situations in the law office, was one thing, but the pressures in his marriage and the festering wounds from his father's disappearance, proved to be too much.

"I thought I had it under control. That's when my anger toward the whole world set in, and that's when it became debilitating. I had been able to keep myself under such good control and handle my life, but I wasn't able to control my life during that period of 1988 through 1992. One of the reasons I did so well in the earlier stages of my life is I was always so busy. I really was the world's busiest guy."

Anita said Al's breakdown took her by surprise.

"I had no clue. I thought it was just age-related. I was very naïve in many ways. At the time, I didn't know anyone who went to a psychologist or psychiatrist. That's how far removed it was. I was a poor kid from Kinsman."

Rachel remembers she was in the fourth grade when she realized her father was sick, but says she knew he didn't have anything like a broken arm. She recalls celebrating her fifth birthday with her dad at the psych unit at Mt. Sinai. The girls remember hearing their parents argue after they had gone to bed at night, but Lottie says she never saw him present his mental illness like she sees with her clients now.

Lottie is a social worker with an agency called Recovery Resources. She deals with mentally ill people who have been charged, but not convicted of felonies. Her experience with her father when she was a child, steered her toward the career.

"It increased my interest in learning about mental illness. My undergraduate major was psychology. My focus in psychology was mental illness. His ordeal piqued my interest. As a child, I really didn't know how sick he was. My mom was able to cover it up pretty well."

Al gives a lot of credit to Dr. Ernest Friedman. Al says Friedman convinced Al to finally come to grips with the fact that his father was likely killed by the gamblers he owed money. The doctor told Al he shouldn't think his constant harping about his dad's gambling was what drove his father away.

"Dr. Friedman asked questions that brought me to the conclusion. At some point, he figured it out. I had ignored the reality that my dad went out to his car to sleep to avoid the gamblers."

Al says the doctors who treated him at Mt. Sinai were good guys and good doctors, but they couldn't get to the root of his problem. He says Dr. Friedman was on to it rather quickly.

Lottie said, "It is very unusual to have an onset of mental illness that late in life."

Anita said she never saw the mental troubles coming. When they took hold of Al, that was it. She believes the festering trauma of his father's disappearance was the cause of his breakdown.

During the final month of his stay at Laurelwood, Al had made enough progress that he was allowed to go home after breakfast each day.

After he was discharged, Al would not return to the family home to live. Firing the gun that day months before, signaled the end of his marriage. He moved into a motel room near Chagrin Boulevard.

Al had not only touched the lives of the other patients at Laurelwood, but members of the staff as well. Every day, he would share stories about the early days of Cleveland. Anecdotes about the war years. Stories about sports. Insights into government and law. Al was the host of the afternoon men's group at the hospital.

"I became a star at Laurelwood. I had a positive effect there."

Al's lifetime friend Harold Mendes said, "He was becoming a lawyer for half the people at Laurelwood. He was the in-house lawyer. He continued to have relationships with a lot of those people. He was an advocate for a lot of the people he met there."

Rachel says attitudes were different about mental illness two decades ago.

"Even if you knew a lot of people who were getting counseling, they probably didn't talk about it back then as much."

Al says his stay at Laurelwood was the longest of any patient there. He says the bill totaled $178,000.

Lottie said, "It was hard to explain to people why he was in the hospital so long and why we were going as many times as we were. Our friends were hanging out and doing kid stuff. In a way, it forced us to cope with more of an adult situation. I'm glad we went, because it made such a difference for him."

Anita said, "I really believe he needed to see his children. He had lost so much at that point. I don't think hiding all of this from them was the way to go."

Bob Luria said, "I think his recovery is pretty remarkable from where he was. That he can function as well as he does today is pretty amazing."

Bob says Al is just a bit different now.

"A lot of his personality is the same. His sense of humor certainly is. He always had a good sense of humor, but he is a lot mellower than he was then. He remembers a lot of things, but there are some periods he has blocked out, or doesn't remember."

Keith Belkin said, "If you would have known how bad he was, he was pretty bad, and to see how he is now, it's pretty impressive."

Once Al was released from Laurelwood, he chose to talk openly about his experience. Jordan Rothkopf said he would bring it up to people he didn't even know.

Jordan said, "Initially, it was troubling. He was always talking about it. Maybe a little too much."

It was during his recovery, that Al attended a fundraiser at Camp Ho Mita Koda in Newbury. It's a place for children who have diabetes. Dinner tents had been set up for the 300 guests in attendance that night.

Arlene Fine, a reporter for the *Cleveland Jewish News* was there at the fundraiser.

"We all went into tents to eat dinner, and of all the tents, Al Gray wound up sitting next to me at the table where I was seated."

Until that evening, Arlene had never met Al. She had heard of him, but they were total strangers. She introduced herself and let him know she was a reporter.

"I had never had a connection with him. He started to tell me his experience with bi-polar depression, and his climb back to sanity. It was a compelling story. I told him I would like to write about it for our readers."

Al told Arlene he was eager to share his story. They spent hours together. Arlene chronicled the depths of his despair and his journey to recovery.

"He was so emphatic that the reason he was sharing this epic story was not for a cathartic effect. He didn't need that. It was to help other people. He was sincere about that."

After the story was published, Al started getting calls from people who said they had a family member who was suffering from depression. They were seeking advice. Al would spend hours on the phone with people trying to offer them some counseling.

Arlene said, "These people were strangers. He was helping them and perhaps even saving lives along the way. I thought it was brave of Al to be so open because there's a stigma attached to mental illness. It's still a little scary if you are in a room and someone says, 'I'm mentally unstable.' You are kind of looking around for the exit."

His stay at Laurelwood changed Al's outlook on many things.

Al said, "It took me a while after Laurelwood to realize how difficult it is for the public to be informed on mental health issues. People were reluctant to talk about it. Whenever I was invited to speak publicly, I would always talk openly about it. Shortly after I was released from the hospital, I went to a meeting of the Jewish Community Federation. I got up and said it's great to be back after five months at Laurelwood. I just decided to say it because if I was reluctant to mention it, it was assumed I was just off in the woods somewhere. Mental illness was never a topic that was delved into in much detail. It's only in recent years people have been willing to talk about it."

Stephen Hoffman, the president of the Jewish Community Federation, said, "Al's never giving up. He's always moving forward, dealing with what life throws at all of us. Things that would have put most people on their knees. In Al's case, he has been able to stay on his feet and keep moving in a very positive forward direction. I think it was the love of his children, and always wanting to be there for them, that gave him the determination to overcome everything."

Lottie said, "A lot of people don't understand mental illness until it affects your family."

When Al was honored by the Jewish fraternity Zeta Beta Tau at its national convention in 2009, he took the opportunity to speak about his battle with mental illness.

Rachel said, "He still acknowledges it, and every time he speaks in public, he always brings it up. He is not ashamed or embarrassed by it. He doesn't try to hide it. After the ZBT luncheon, someone came up to him and said, 'I just want to thank you, because I suffer from mental illness, and it really means a lot to me that you mentioned it.'"

Anita says Al's recovery was indeed an accomplishment.

"He was really sick. The fact this man has come so far, is absolutely amazing. He was hearing voices. He was really sick."

Rachel thinks her dad relied on his inner strengths to fight his way back.

"Because he is so stubborn, because he's been through everything he's been through, I think that pointed him toward success. I don't think any of us could say, when he got out of the hospital, he was completely fine. That's not how it works. It's not like he never had ups and downs after that. He struggled after that period. I think it's something that is always with you to some extent. I think because he loved his family so much, he knew he had to be well for his family. He didn't want to lose Lottie and me. He didn't want to lose the relationship he had with any of us, and I think he knew, unless he got better, he would."

Rachel's boyfriend Geoff Hanks says most prominent people dealing with a mental breakdown, would try to keep things quiet, not let people know.

"When it hits a professional in the prime of his career who is definitely respected in the community, it's not the guy walking down the street talking to himself, picking up cans. Bringing that out in the public eye in the '80s and '90s helped out a lot of people. Look how far we have come with mental illness in the last twenty-five years. If it were not for people like Al coming out and talking about it, we wouldn't have made as much progress. Mental illness affects a lot of people out there. This is a serious medical issue."

Al said, "I have had a high degree of recovery, which is rare. I don't underestimate what it means to be able to function almost as fully as you would like, in fact, I think I do function as well as I like. Considering all my limitations, I have been able to deal with my lifestyle pretty effectively."

Al is grateful he has been able to overcome his demons.

"I think about it every day. I wake up with gratitude, and go to sleep every night with affection for my life. A lot of guys at eighty-one don't have personal trainers, don't have a bank account, don't have a family. As things are, I feel great. I have never been in a hospital for a physical reason other than for an overnight test. That's pretty darn good. I think it's great to wake up every morning and feel great, and I do. I want to see my kids, and I think they want to see me."

Since his recovery, some observers might not think Al's behavior is totally mainstream. He is a flamboyant, if not outrageous kind of guy. Reflecting on his tough times is part of his daily routine.

"None of us should forget our personal history, and I sure don't forget mine. I think I have learned to deal with it pretty well. Perfectly? No."

Rita Gray Newman said about her cousin's recovery, "A lot of people can't talk about things that have happened to them. For him to share what has happened, and to show positive results that can come from all of this, he's affecting a lot of people who might feel frustrated, or not knowing what to do, or feeling they are going to give up. He's showing that you don't give up. You don't quit. It's easy to give up with anything that happens to you."

Rita is impressed by her cousin's unrelenting determination.

"I think he's amazing. His strength. To be so determined. To once again become involved as a father. To pull his life together. It's so good he has been able to reach out to so many people. He has affected so many people. He's come back from all sorts of experiences and pulled himself up to be a good person."

Dr. Ernest Friedman

Dr. Ernest Friedman is seated in a wheelchair in the living room of his condominium in Beachwood. He is dressed casually, wearing a denim shirt and blue jeans. A pair of slippers is on his feet. Just shy of eighty, he still has a full head of gray hair. His movements are limited, yet you can tell this is an imposing man.

He jokes about the first time Al Gray came into his psychiatry office on Forest Hills Boulevard in East Cleveland.

"I went into practice in 1962, so I had a twenty-year gestation period to get ready for Al. I knew there had to be something waiting for me at the end of the tunnel. It was Al. A lot of people never find anything at the end of the tunnel. I gave Al a relationship. It was life-saving for him."

Dr. Friedman took a measured approach with Al. He took baby steps. Blasting ahead full speed would have been unproductive.

"You had to know when to key in, and when to key out. He had trepidations. I had to be circumspect. I very, very carefully built up a relationship."

Dr. Friedman knew Al had fired that gunshot in his yard in Shaker Heights, but said he wasn't afraid of him. His first priority was getting Al away from his low point. He described the situation as dicey.

"He was in a quandary. He had his problems, and he wasn't resolving them. He had been through the mill. You don't see a strong recovery like his too often. I spent a lot of time with him going through his life history and seeking a clarification of what was going on. That didn't come easily. I did a lot of listening."

Al was put on medications to ease his mental instability. Dr. Friedman says that was a vital step. He says that was an non-negotiable item. The therapy sessions were by no means routine.

"His being an attorney meant each session I had with him was like another Supreme Court case. He argued his position forcefully. It was like going into a courtroom. I had to tread carefully because he was queasy about me slapping a psychiatric diagnosis on him."

Ernest Friedman had the feeling that Al always had something up his sleeve.

"In a patient like this, there is a big danger of being seduced. I was watching this very carefully to see when the seduction came. He had a fine mind. He was like a bejeweled timepiece. Some people would see him as very charming. He would see himself as in command. Who was going to compete with him?"

What caused Al to become manic-depressive? Dr. Friedman says genetics may have played a role. He says there can be a ticking time bomb in a person's genetic makeup. He says Al's relationship with his father may have been a factor, but he doesn't discount the possibility that Al's marriage complicated matters for him.

"It disclosed certain problems. Ultimately the truth came out for Anita. She was married to a man who had something wrong with him. He had interpersonal stress. He had a problem settling into a marital situation."

Al had been accustomed to an independent life. He remained single until age forty-seven. He was twenty years older than Anita. They loved each other, but Dr. Friedman speculated that Al grew jealous of Anita.

"Her star was rising at the Jewish Community Federation, and Al was left in a secondary role. That was a collision. It was only a matter of time before things fell apart."

Dr. Friedman says the bullet Al fired was kind of like a warning shot, but it could have gotten more serious.

"You never know. You don't know who is going to be around the next day. The stockpiling of guns was inappropriate hyper-activity. Anything is possible with this illness. We took Al out a stressful window, being in a difficult situation in terms of his marriage. So that problem resolved rather quickly. He seemed anxious to get better."

Ernest Friedman and Al Gray, each the smartest guy in the room, found themselves together in one room. It was a match made in heaven. Ernest had the intellectual savvy to go toe-to-toe with Al. He unlocked the mystery that had overtaken Al's life. He became a friend. A confidant.

"I don't think he had any escape valve with his family members. It became very important for us to maintain our connection, and we did maintain it. He probably never had that connection with his family. Relatives didn't know what to do. They want to help, but they don't know how, nor should we expect them to know."

Al gives Ernest Friedman full credit for his recovery. The doctor is not one to bask in the glow.

"I don't get carried with anything like that. He can butter people up. I was aware I had to watch my step, so that I wouldn't get sucked into his mishegas. So I played it as objectively as I could."

Does Ernest at least feel proud of his meaningful work with Al?

"The pride comes before the fall. That is the last thing I would look for. Being proud. No way. The jury is usually still out. I don't want to give anybody any false hope and take credit where no credit is due, so the secret is to be very humble."

Strip Search

L ong before Al's mental illness took hold of his life, Al became deeply involved in the battle to free Soviet Jews from lives of oppression. Anita Gray joined her husband in this human rights struggle.

In February of 1978, Al and Anita traveled to Moscow. The purpose of the trip was to witness the trial of Soviet dissident Natan Sharansky. Sharansky was one of the leading figures in the Refusenik movement in the Soviet Union. A Refusenik was a Soviet Jew who wanted to leave the country. Once he or she had applied for a visa, they were subject to various forms of harassment. Sharansky had applied for an exit visa in 1973. That request was denied, and Sharansky, like other Soviet Jews who eagerly sought freedom, risked being sent to a labor camp in Siberia.

Upon arrival in the Soviet Union, Al and Anita discovered the beginning of the trial had been pushed back. So they decided to meet with other Refuseniks in order to better understand their plight. They met with a young man whose wife was a doctor. He had written a letter to a newspaper about his wife being denied a visa.

Al told the man he wanted a copy of that letter. It wasn't exactly a top secret document. After all, it had already been published in the newspaper.

Al and Anita were given a copy, and carried it with them to Leningrad. Instead of transporting the letter back to the United States, Al thought it was best to present it to the U.S. Consul there, so its safety could be assured.

"The next day we went to the airport at 9 a.m. The KGB grabbed our suitcases and went through everything. They didn't find anything. They slit the lining of the suitcases and when they didn't find anything, they strip-searched us."

Anita said, "You haven't lived until you have been strip-searched by the KGB. They grilled us. We were at the airport four hours before the vice-consul showed up to help us. I knew I was clean, and I knew Al was clean, but what I didn't know was if they were going to plant something on us. I just had no trust of any of them."

By the time the interrogation was over, Al and Anita had missed their flight.

Anita said, "We came this close to being arrested."

The vice-consul, Oscar Clyatt, told them to return to their hotel, and in order to limit their exposure, urged them not to leave their room.

Clyatt promised to pick them up in the morning and drive them back to the airport. When Clyatt went to his car the next morning, it had a flat tire. No doubt it had been punctured by the KGB. He then got another car from the U.S. Embassy in order to take Al and Anita to the airport.

Anita said, "On the drive to the airport, Clyatt didn't say a word. I said, 'Oscar don't you think we should talk about what happened yesterday?'"

He said, "Sure Anita, as long as you know this car is probably bugged."

Al Takes on the KGB

⁓※⁓

Al had an earlier brush with the KGB. The year was 1967. Al was planning his second trip to the Soviet Union. He applied for a passport. Al wanted to visit Siberia on this trip in order to see a part of the world he had not yet seen.

"I got a call from a man who said he was with the CIA. We arranged for him to visit me in my law office. He asked me if I would be willing to take pictures of a dam being constructed in Siberia. He told me the satellite they had orbiting the Earth wasn't able to get pictures of the dam. They wanted to see what the dam looked like."

The dam was supposed to be the largest in the world. This would be Al's first exposure to spying and international intrigue.

"I said let me think about it. Two minutes later, I said okay. I think you have to believe in what you are doing. If it scares the hell out of you, don't do it. If it scared me, I wouldn't do it. I knew the consequences were potentially dangerous. So what the hell."

Al followed through with his promise. He stood outside the dam and started snapping pictures. A man approached. In broken English, identified himself as an officer of the KGB.

"I am taking photographs."

"Why are you taking photographs?"

"I have a hobby of taking photographs."

"Give me your camera."

Al had another roll of film in his pocket. The officer ordered Al to come with him. Al followed him into a small hut.

"There was a table and two chairs. He locked the door behind me."

Al pondered his fate. Would he be formally interrogated? Would he be detained for a long period of time?

"Years later, I found out the officer had called his boss and the KGB called Moscow. They had a red phone and the Kremlin called the White House. The White House and the Kremlin decided they didn't want this to be an international incident. They determined they should release me and return my camera and film. The whole episode took several hours. When I got back to the United States, I gave the film to the CIA."

So how did Al find out that his dam photos warranted a call on the hot line?

"Three years later, my name was in the newspapers because of my activism for Jewish causes. A woman wrote a letter threatening to kill my wife, my children and me. I contacted the FBI. They told me the woman was harmless. At that point, they had looked through the file on me, and told me what they had regarding that 1967 Siberian incident."

Coming to America

Al's ancestry can be traced back to Europe. He proudly wears a diamond ring on his right pinkie. The ring has a lot of symbolic meaning for him.

"My grandparents came here from Poland in December of 1892. My grandfather, Louis Griafski, was able to smuggle this diamond in. My uncle eventually had it set in this ring."

Louis and his wife Katie Griafski were not alone. They came to America with their only child at the time, one-month-old Rob. He would be the first of seven children. Eight years after settling here, the family name was Americanized to Gray.

Louis made a living by peddling soda-pop on the streets of Cleveland. He traveled around town in a horse-drawn wagon. Al has the original recipes for the soda-pop, and takes great pride in having them.

Al's mother Lottie Weingarden was born in Chicago. Her parents, Joseph and Bessie Weingarden had come to America from Poland just two years after Louis and Katie Griafski did.

Al's father Rob was only twenty-three years old when he joined forces with his brother Irwin to buy the Wood Transfer and Moving Company. The business hit pay-dirt when large numbers of Jewish residents of Cleveland's Glenville neighborhood started moving up the hill to Cleveland Heights. The company was housed in a small, one-story, metal building on Mayfield Road, just west of Coventry. Al remembers it got terribly cold inside that building in the winter time. The trucks were parked in a nearby garage.

Al's grandfather Louis died in 1911. Louis's wife Katie continued to live in their house on Columbia, near E. 105th Street. Al's Aunt Cel and Uncle Hy were unmarried and they continued to live with their mother in that house. Al and his parents would drive to the Glenville neighborhood once a week to visit his grandmother, but during the observance of the Jewish New Year, the family would actually stay there.

"We stayed over-night because my father didn't think it was right to drive a car over the two days of Rosh Hashana. So we took baskets, large baskets, not suitcases, but laundry baskets loaded with our clothing."

The temple was located at the corner of Tacoma and E.105th. People in the neighborhood called it Tacoma Shul.

Al's grandfather Louis was barely forty years old when he died. He apparently developed some sort of illness after attending the funeral of his best friend. Al's father Rob accepted the role as the head of the extended family. He didn't shirk his responsibilities. He helped send two of his brothers to dental school, and put another brother through college.

One of the brothers who became a dentist was Morris Gray. Morris and his wife Fannie had two children, Rita and Alan. For Al Gray to have a first cousin named Alan Gray, there was some degree of confusion. Rita tried to minimize the confusion over the years by affectionately calling her cousin Alvie.

Rita, who is about a year younger than her cousin, said, "He was wonderful as a cousin. The families got together every Sunday over at our grandmother's house on Columbia Avenue. All the cousins, all the uncles and all the aunts were there. Passover was always huge. Everyone was there."

Ruth Gray was married to Al's brother Louis. She remembers the family spent a lot of time together, but matters were not always peaceful.

She said, "They didn't all get along. They were hot-tempered. They were excitable."

Adam Fried is a forty-year-old attorney in Cleveland. His grandmother Cecile was one of Rob Gray's sisters. He gives Al a lot of credit for staying committed to keeping the bonds strong with the extended family.

"In his generation, all of the extended family lived in the same neighborhood, and so they all knew each other. It was the same with my father's generation. They had cousins clubs. They spent time together. As people moved to different locations, you started seeing each other on an infrequent basis. The next generation didn't even know each other. The fact that Al keeps in touch with me, shows he has an affinity for family."

Al devoted much of his childhood to playing baseball. When he lived on Silsby, there was a vacant lot just east of Lee Road. Al and the neighborhood guys transformed it into a makeshift ball field.

Al was thrilled when he was given a Mickey Mouse flip-book when he was four years old. Flip through the pages, and it looked like Mickey was flying an airplane. Al says his love of aviation may have started with that simple book.

Al's first job was working at Amster Drug. It was located at Taylor Road and Superior Park Drive. Abe Amster had opened the store in 1933. It overlooked a ravine which was later transformed into Cain Park. The store was by no means fancy.

Al said, "It was a piece of junk, that's what it looked like. The store was about thirty feet deep. Everything was in showcases. It could be described as a "shtoonky" store. Abe was a little tyrannical. Not a bad guy, but not a personality. I learned from him how not to treat your help."

Al was fourteen years old when he worked at Amster for the summer and fall of 1942. He was paid twenty-five cents an hour. He would work about five and a half hours per shift, earning a little more than a dollar-twenty-five for his efforts.

"My mother thought it was a good idea to have a job. She felt it was a safe store in a neighborhood not far from home. She knew the owner."

Al tried his hand at selling *Collier's* magazine door to door. He earned half a cent on each magazine he sold. He also earned bonus points. When he accumulated enough, he was awarded a baseball bat. He still has that bat. He eventually got a paper route as well.

In his teenage years, Al would meet his buddies at Ralph's poolroom. It was just south of the Cedar-Lee theater and was in the basement. The owner was Ralph Gervasi. He was bald, had a sizeable nose and a big belly. Ralph reminded Al of his father.

"Ralph didn't know how to treat us. It's not that he was impolite. He was a nice guy. He would always say, 'Don't bounce-ah duh cue ball.'"

Al's brother Louis was ten years older, so the two brothers weren't particularly close. Lou's girlfriend Ruth Pollack lived in the Glenville neighborhood. He spent a great deal of time with her. Lou was less of a free spirit than Al was. He tended to be more serious. Lou went to pharmacy school at Ohio Northern, and after a stint in the Army during the war, he found work as a pharmacist. He would eventually own a couple of drugstores. The last store he owned was at E. 105th and Superior. Lou decided to abandon the store after the Hough riots in the '60s.

At the end of eighth grade at Roxboro Junior High, Al perfected the art of playing both ends against the middle. A candidate for Student Council President asked Al to write his campaign speech for him.

"Ronnie Barth asked me first, before Joe Spicuzza became a candidate. I said sure. We were good friends and in the same homeroom. We played ball together. I wrote a nice little speech for him. Spicuzza became interested in running later, and he was a better friend of mine. So, when he asked me to write his speech, I had no hesitancy. So, I wrote both speeches."

Spicuzza won the election. Decades later, both of the candidates died within a month of each other.

It was the fall of 1942 when Al stepped into Cleveland Heights High for the first time.

"It was a little overwhelming compared to Roxboro. The war was going on and I was interested in the war, weapons, and airplanes. My schoolwork suffered that first year. I went on to have good grades later, but my tenth grade marks were not good. I evolved into my own form of war strategist. I did pay a tremendous amount of attention to Germany's invasion of Poland. I was a history buff. A military buff. I knew all models of tanks and airplanes. I knew what the uniforms looked like."

Al was the sportswriter at Roxboro and continued that at Heights High, but his interest in pursuing journalism as a career was already fading.

"We did vocational research in ninth grade at Roxboro. I rejected journalism when I learned that the average journalist was making 900 dollars a year. When my social studies teacher Walter Kincaid told me that, I changed my plans. Decades later, after I had become a successful lawyer, I wound up living in the same neighborhood as Mr. Kincaid. I reminded him he was responsible for discouraging me from being a journalist. 'You haven't done too badly by going into law,' he said."

Al said many of his friends from Heights pursued careers in medicine, but it was his time working in the kitchen at boot camp, after his Navy pre-flight training, that put an end to that.

"I didn't like working with chicken gizzards and figured medicine wasn't for me. I figured law was exciting. So many of our great accomplishments have related to law. During the Depression years, lawyers were low wage earners, so I didn't think in terms of money when I made my career choice."

Money issues were always a consideration during Al's childhood.

"It was an ongoing condition. We always lived in a rental. My dad drove a Packard, but it was always a used Packard. We lived a moderate life. It wasn't a poor life, it was a modest life."

Al has fond memories of Mawby's restaurant near Cedar and Lee.

"It was the place for a ten-cent hamburger. It was all counter. A really long counter that was cut in the middle so they could get back behind the counter. French fries were probably five cents. You could eat there for about twenty cents plus one cent tax. The floor was black and white tile."

Further north on Lee Road was Clark's restaurant. It was part of a chain. It was priced well with decent food. Al says it catered to families. The children who cleaned their plates got a trip to the treasure chest and could select a toy.

Al spent his earliest of years living in an apartment in the Glenville area on Lynn Drive. The family lived there until Al was four.

"The streets were narrow, brick, and bumpy. East 105th had streetcar tracks in the middle. There was a good bit of traffic, parking was tight."

Al has fond memories of a couple of Jewish delicatessens not far from his grandmother's home in Glenville. Barney's featured more dinner items than Solomon's did. Glenville was a vibrant Jewish community, but times were difficult.

"In the '30s, everyone had to be tough because of the Depression. It was a tough era. There were strong negative feelings."

Al's mother had a limited budget to work with, but always made sure the family was well fed. Considering the rough economic times, his father's business was able to hold its own. Most people had a hard time finding work.

Al was an avid reader as a young man. The presidential campaign of Franklin Roosevelt in 1940 was a big deal for him.

"Roosevelt took a good view of the world. He spoke out against German oppression. The news reports and my parents conversations convinced me Roosevelt did a good job of getting us out of the Depression. My dad always used to joke about when I was with adults, I'd talk about adult things, just as they did. They would laugh about it. I knew so much about adult issues. Even at age twelve, I was well-informed. I read the newspaper cover to cover. I thought Roosevelt was fabulous. He was going to get us out of the Depression. I wasn't anxious for the United States to be in the war, but I was positive about how good we were as a country. I was really proud of our country. I was a strong supporter of our way of life."

Al's feeling about the war would soon change. He was a member of a high school fraternity called AA Junior. On December 7, 1941 Al and six other club members gathered at a friend's home for a meeting.

"At some point, when the meeting was ending, we got the news about the attack on Pearl Harbor. It was an overwhelming announcement. Only one or two pictures of the attack were released right away. But one year later, *Life* magazine carried vivid pictures. At first, the government didn't want the public to know the extent of damage and wanted to maintain secrecy."

Al can recall the days when the Warrensville and Cedar area was largely undeveloped. The apartments along Cedar were not built yet. There was a drive-in style restaurant called Lenny's. He says there were small spaces to park your car. It was on the south side of Cedar, just west of Warrensville. Owner Lenny Union served hamburgers and French fries there.

"He had been in the Army. He blinked a lot. He knew how to make hamburgers. Lenny's was there for perhaps fifteen years. He ran the place for six or seven years. There were small tables inside and a small counter. For its era, the food was pretty good. Very good French fries."

Al was never very big in stature. At his peak, he stood a little more than five-foot-five. When he went out on dates, Al was able to borrow his dad's Packard. He seems to remember the front seat was in a fixed position. It could not be adjusted. Al had to sit forward in order to reach the gas pedal and peer over the steering wheel.

"I used to love to drive on a date to the Shanghai restaurant on Rockwell Avenue. The pricing was good, The food was good. A meal cost 35 cents. Gas was only 15.9 cents a gallon. Even back then, I knew my way around Cleveland. That's one of the reasons I have been unfailingly loyal to Cleveland. Through good and bad times, I just like living here. It was called the sixth city back then because it was the sixth biggest city in the United States."

By the time Al got married at age forty-seven, his cousins had been married for years. He had already worked for more than twenty years as a lawyer. Al put in long hours. His work was his primary focus. During those years, he was a bit disconnected from relatives.

His sister-in-law, Ruth Gray said, "In his younger years, other family members were settling down and having children. He was still single. As he grew older, he became more aware of family. He started making efforts to stay in touch."

Ruth's daughter, Carol Marger, says Al's commitment to family has remained strong. Carol lives in Florida, but Al stays in close contact with her and her three children, Eli, Meg, and Bernard.

"I think family is very important to Al. He's shown a lot of interest, affection and support. He is always interested in what we do. He always offers us advice. He is a generous man. He likes family. He loves family. My children are very fond of him. I like talking to Al. I like listening to Al. We talk about what matters in life. He has been a shaping factor in my life."

Uncle Hy

When Al was a young boy and his family was spending the two-day Rosh Hashanah holiday at his grandmother's house in Glenville, he would share a bedroom with his Uncle Hy. Hy was unmarried and still living with his mother on Columbia Avenue. It was a modest childhood for Hy, but even back then, he was a generous guy. He would give a dollar to his nephew Al whenever he saw him.

Hy landed a job with Weinberger Drug. The primary store was located at E.105th and Euclid. It was open twenty-four hours a day. That was uncommon eighty years ago. By today's standards, the store was small, but for its day, it was huge.

Al said, "It was a nice place to go. So much there. So many candy bars. The store had a soda fountain. The fixtures and shelves had a look that reflected the era."

Adolph Weinberger opened his original store in Cleveland in 1912. It was located at E. 30th and Scovill. The Weinberger chain grew to seven stores in Cleveland. Adolph Weinberger recognized that his employee Hy Gray had plenty of talent and allowed him to lead an ambitious expansion of the chain.

37

Stores were acquired in Pennsylvania and New York. Stores were added throughout Ohio. The chain took on the name Gray Drug.

Al said, "That was an easier name to take to a small town, because in the '30s and '40s there were still anti-Jewish feelings in small towns, especially among people who had little contact with Jews. With the Depression and pessimism running rampant, the world was dominated by anti-Semitism. There would be people who didn't want to work for a Jewish company, and there were people who didn't want to buy from a Jewish company. People knew which companies were Jewish-owned. That kind of thing had a way of being known back then."

Hy Gray was consumed with his role at Gray Drug. He didn't take time to marry until 1952 when he was forty-nine years old. He drove new, fancy cars.

"He was too busy to get married. He was a kind, generous man, but a tough businessman. He had instinct. He had background. He had a good reputation. He knew a good bit about the world. Adolph Weinberger credited him with building the chain. He was the executive vice president of the company."

Al says Gray Drug was known for treating its employees well. They were able to keep good workers on the payroll.

"One of the best things he could do was walk into a drugstore and tell the head pharmacist exactly what to do to correct things in the store. He was usually very accurate in his evaluation."

The Gray Drug chain expanded dramatically by taking over the Drug Fair chain. It wound up being sold off to Rite Aid. Al says Uncle Hy was a well-respected man. He died in 1987 and left a fortune of three million dollars.

Deep Friendships

While a student at Cleveland Heights High School, Al started developing friendships that would go on to last a lifetime. He has always treasured those friendships.

More than sixty years after graduation, Al set out to attend the funeral of his high school pal, Arthur Fitzmartin. Al's drive to the Western Reserve National Cemetery in Rittman would cover nearly fifty miles.

"I was the only high school friend who showed up for that."

Arthur Fitzmartin had been a Marine. He was being buried with full military honors.

"He was a lively kind of guy. He lived near me during high school. When I couldn't get my father's Packard, Art would drive. He had his own car. An old Ford."

Art had done all right with an insulation business he ran in Cleveland. He married three times. His relationship with his children was not always smooth.

Art was nearly eighty years old when he called Al, Harold Mendes, and Alan Schonberg. They were his friends from high school. Art said he was in Panama. He said he was down and out. He was involved in a situation there, and asked if they could help him by sending some money.

Al agreed to send him some.

"He was a friend for a lot of years. I have had friends who have had ups and downs, and I try to be supportive. I thought people were very supportive of me during my seven months in mental hospitals. It was no big deal. I write checks to philanthropy all the time. To write one for a friend who calls me from Panama for a little bit of money is no big deal."

Harold Mendes view of Arthur was not as glowing.

"Art was a selfish guy. I accepted him for what he was. He was out for himself."

Harold didn't open his checkbook for Arthur, but doesn't fault Al for helping out.

"He has a sense of loyalty to old, old friends."

Al said Arthur eventually made his way back to Ohio and moved in with his son. That didn't work out too well, and he got an apartment near University Circle. Al said the janitor noticed a flood of water. Arthur had suffered a heart attack while taking a shower. He died there.

Leonard Scharfeld was another Heights High classmate.

"I went to his funeral even though I had sued him."

Al and Leonard were both lawyers. They shared an office in the Superior Building from 1953 to 1975. They weren't partners, just office mates. Al paid the salary of a woman who served as office manager. She did some work for Leonard, but was technically Al's employee. Al was stunned to discover she was embezzling money. He figured the loss at $42,000. She was prosecuted, and was put on probation. Al and his wife Anita couldn't believe what happened. They had considered the woman a friend.

"I went to Leonard and asked him to contribute some money to make up for the loss. He wouldn't contribute a dime. I asked if he could cover ten percent of the loss. He said no."

The lease for the office was nearing an end. Al told Leonard he would be moving to another office.

"Leonard asked where are we going to go. I said, honey, the marriage is over."

About five years before the break up, Leonard's brother-in-law Dick Klaus had purchased a radio station in Kent called WKNT. Al invested $10,000 in the venture.

"Leonard and Dick owned 80 percent of the stock and they sold twenty percent to the public in 1970. I was the largest minority stockholder. They had a big profit in 1981 of half a million dollars. The majority stockholders took a vote and took half of those profits and put the rest into operating funds for the radio station. We got zero. You can't do that to minority shareholders."

Al confronted Leonard and asked him why he was driving him to file a lawsuit against him.

Leonard said, "Do what you have to do."

Al was enraged and more inspired than ever to take legal action.

Al said, "I'm going to Florida for a week. Think it over."

Leonard told Al he was also going to Florida for a week, and he didn't have to think it over.

Al decided to press on with the suit. How did he feel about suing a lifelong friend and longtime office mate?

"Sad, very sad. About as sad as a guy can feel. As sad as I would have felt if a woman I loved and I was married to, had been unfaithful. That's how bad I felt."

Filing suit against Leonard Scharfeld was one the most difficult steps Al took in his life, but he had a strategy.

"I went to an attorney named Wilton Sogg and hired him. I knew he didn't get along with Scharfeld. I figured why not irritate Scharfeld even more."

Al said the case wound up being settled in just nineteen days. He says Scharfeld admitted he had been a fool to encourage Al to sue him. Al was awarded a settlement of $329,000. The other minority shareholders were also compensated.

Once the settlement was reached, Al didn't want to hate Scharfeld.

"I considered the case was closed. I try to eliminate animosity in my thinking. My experience in the mental hospitals taught me to deal with animosity. It takes an enormous amount now for me to really hold a grudge. At my age, if you are going to do it now, you are going to worry yourself out of the world. You have to focus on what you need to focus on, and get rid of the rest."

Al's friendship with Harold Mendes has lasted more than sixty-five years. He claims Harold walked into Amster Drug one day while Al was working there. Harold was going to Roosevelt Junior High and Al was going to Roxboro. They would be entering Heights High that fall. Harold has no memory of them meeting that summer, but remembers meeting Al's father before he met Al.

"In 1939, my family was moving from Lakeview Road in Cleveland to Antisdale in Cleveland Heights. Al's father and his Uncle Irwin handled the move for us. His dad was stocky and muscular. I can still visualize seeing him taking things off the truck. I can see him smoking a cigar. He wasn't afraid of work. Those guys worked."

Harold said he and Al were in the same club at Heights High.

"He always had a lot of girls around him. He and Alan Schonberg were kind of wild guys, always chasing women."

Al said Harold has been a steadying influence on him over the decades.

"He was very sincere, but not a super-outgoing kind of guy. He has integrity. An ability to judge people. He is terribly responsible. He wore well as a friend. He has a willingness to be helpful. He changed my life when he introduced me to Japanese stocks."

Al plunged into those Japanese stocks way ahead of the pack and he deftly maneuvered out of them in a skillful manner.

Geoff Greenleaf, of Private Harbour Investment Management, said, "Fortunately with his Japanese stocks, he didn't hold them all the way down. The Japanese market peaked twenty years ago. It was at 39,000 on their Dow, and now it's down to 10,500. That market has lost almost

75% in the last 25 years. They have had a horrible, long bear market, and Al has basically avoided that."

Harold recognizes Al was skilled as a lawyer.

"He did very well. He was a patient guy. He didn't have his hand out right away. He didn't say I won't do any work for you unless you give me five hundred dollars up front. He got along with people. He was a capable guy. He was a good negotiator. He could settle things. I don't think he was mean and nasty. He tried to ameliorate things. He was a bright guy."

In the early '50s, Harold worked for Muntz TV. Bob Beni and Art Gartman ran the store at E.71st and Euclid. They told Harold they were looking for a lawyer. Harold recommended Al.

"It turned into a bonanza for Al cause these guys were constantly getting into trouble. Lease issues. Family divorces. They were a couple of characters."

Al said, "Bob and Art were a lot of fun. Grownups who liked to have fun. Gartman was more of family guy. Beni was more social. Beni was the ultimate of wild guys. In Hollywood, he would have been a director who made love with all of his stars. Bob Beni was from Collinwood. That was a very important part of his life. He could have been mayor of Collinwood. Because of him, I developed a great following in the Collinwood neighborhood."

Al didn't mind getting attention.

"I thought of myself as a neighborhood lawyer. I liked it. I liked walking down 9th Street and everybody calling out, 'Hi, Al.' The Hickory Grill, Kornman's and the Theatrical. If I walked into those places, people would say, 'Hi, Mr. Gray, or hi, Al.'"

Harold admits Al can be stubborn and overbearing at times.

"He was upset when Bernice Rube was selected for the Cleveland Heights High Hall of Fame before he was. He doesn't mind being in the spotlight. I accept him for what he is. He's got faults. I've got faults."

Harold knows from time to time, Al will show up at a social event dressed in a questionable manner.

"There was a time he was wearing Vietnamese pajamas. He can be strange cargo."

In the fall of 1943, Al wandered into Ralph's poolroom. He was by himself. Al had just started eleventh grade at Heights High. The poolroom was a short walk from the school.

A few minutes later, Alan Schonberg arrived. He was a tenth grader at Heights. One of the new kids at the school. Al asked Alan if he wanted to shoot a game.

Al said, "Alan was a pretty interesting guy. Women found him quite attractive. In tenth grade, he started going out with girls who were in eleventh grade. I would say he was a lot sharper than me. I wouldn't say he was smarter than me."

On May 8, 1945, students arrived as usual at Cleveland Heights High, but this would not be a usual day. It was Victory in Europe day. The students would gather in the school auditorium to celebrate the end of the war in Europe. The mood was upbeat, but tempered somewhat by the fact that the war still raged on in the Pacific. The assembly wrapped up by mid-morning.

Al, Howard Perris, Chuck Weiss, and Shael Siegel got into Alan Schonberg's 1935 Ford.

"Alan drove us to South Euclid. They were just developing the streets near Cedar and Warrensville. We pulled onto a street. It may have been Bayard. We had a bottle of something and started drinking."

After that, they drove back to Cedar and Lee. Alan parked his car on Cedar. Everyone except Shael walked around the corner to shoot some pool at Ralph's.

"Shael stayed behind to be with Jackie Kahn. He still had the bottle and started drinking in front of her, just as a police officer drove by. He told the policeman that the rest of his group was down in Ralph's. He went down there and took us all to the Cleveland Heights police station."

Sergeant Batchelor was stationed behind the booking desk. He lived across the street from Al on Silsby.

"Al, what are you doing here?"

"One of the guys told him I was just with the group and I hadn't been drinking. Of course I had been drinking. They had us sit there at the police station and then let us go."

Without a doubt, Al's greatest Heights High caper stemmed from his aversion to taking swimming class. The girls at the school were given bathing suits for swim class. The boys had to swim in their birthday suits.

"I had a thing at that point, of being undressed in front of men. I wasn't interested in doing that. So I decided to break into the school at night. It was a Friday night. I hid in the bushes. My English teacher, Miss Tyler, walked out of the building. She didn't see me. I broke a window and went into the nurse's office. I had an ink eraser. I erased the name on a disability letter from a doctor. It was an excuse to get out of swimming. I substituted my name on the letter. It worked. I got credit for swimming."

Just why did Heights make the boys swim in the buff?

"It's because they didn't want a bunch of wet bathing suits around the locker room. I once asked Roy Uber, the assistant athletic director, why they did that, and he told me it was just a tradition at the school since it was built."

Uber's boss was Gail Vannorsdall.

"It was a strange name for an athletic-looking guy. It made him more fearsome. I think it made him tougher as a result of being named Gail."

Al's friendship with Alan Schonberg has endured sixty-six years. When Alan launched his head-hunting firm, Management Recruiters International, Al was brought on as the original lawyer for the company.

"I helped fashion franchise agreements. It was a new field back in the early '60s. It became enormous. Alan and I got along well. We trusted each other. A lot of handshakes were involved. It did play a part in shaping my life."

Alan, who pronounces his last name as if it were Shone-berg, thinks fondly of Al.

He said, "I couldn't have more regard for him, respect for him, and affection for him. He was good to my children. Generous with my children. I couldn't have had a better relationship with Al."

Al Gray was no doubt a bit envious of Alan Schonberg's success with the ladies at Heights High. Most guys were.

Alan Schonberg said, "Al was not at ease socially at Heights and therefore tried to cover it up with bravado, but Al has been one of the most brilliant people I know. He had flashes of brilliance back in high school, but they didn't get a lot of attention back then. I always had a very warm, open and goomba feeling with him."

Alan Schonberg looks back at his decades with Al before Al's mental breakdown, as halcyon years. Alan was stunned when his friend's behavior turned.

"I never had the slightest inkling he had, or ever would suffer from any psychiatric disturbance, no manic-depression, or paranoia of any sort. I figured he was as stable as stable could be. It never entered my mind that he was anything other than brilliant, stable, hardworking, and considerate. He did a lot for a lot of people, did an enormous amount for the community, and gave of himself."

Alan was consumed with his business obligations, but made the effort to visit Al, at least once a week, during his stay at Laurelwood.

"I felt I needed to support him."

He is proud of Al for his recovery from mental illness, and says Al is confident he is all the way back.

"He feels he is so okay. He feels he can defy convention when he wants. When he walks in looking like Bozo the Clown, or in pajamas, or a jumpsuit, he is defying convention and proving it is okay to do that."

Al was forty years old when he met Bob Silverman. Bob was chairman of the committee at the Jewish Community Federation that was applying pressure on the issue of Soviet Jews. Al had just returned

from one of his early trips to the Soviet Union in support of Refuseniks
there. Al's friendship with Bob has endured since they joined forces on
the issue of Soviet Jews.

Bob said, "Al is very loyal, very generous, and very kind. I don't
think his commitment to Jewish causes could be any greater."

Asked why Al goes out of his way to maintain good friendships, Bob
said, "I imagine the same reason everyone does. Life isn't worthwhile if
you don't have good friends."

Bob and his wife Myrtle have now moved into Stone Gardens, an
assisted living facility in Beachwood. Bob doesn't drive any more. Al
drops by a couple of times a month, for dinner with the Silvermans.

Bob said, "We have an assigned table for dinner. My wife and I sit
with two other men. Al joined us at the table and one of the men was
Don Neuberger. Don recognized Al from his frequent visits to Corky's.
Al knows everybody, or everybody knows him."

Arlene Fine says it's amazing to watch Al in action at a restaurant
like Corky & Lenny's.

"Sometimes I will see him at Corky's with three or four women, and
the waitress will want to sit down and join the group. Very often, he will
go from table to table when all the old-timers are there eating breakfast.
He'll shake hands. He'll make a wisecrack about somebody's hat. He
will talk about a baseball game. If he sees a woman, he will recall that
he dated her in junior high or say he dated her sister."

Arlene says it is not unusual for Al to remember that a particular
woman was "really something" when she was younger.

Arlene said, "He's likeable. He's been around for a long time, already.
He knows so many people. The waitresses and busboys all know him
by name. At Mom's Diner, he told one of the waitresses he has her
Christmas present at his house, and she said she would drop by and
pick it up."

Bob Silverman said, "We were at Moxie for dinner. He wound up at
a half a dozen other tables. He knew this guy, and that guy. Everybody
who came in, knew him."

Bob is dazzled by all of the treasures Al has at his home.

Bob said, "Every time he comes here, he brings something over here, and I have to find some place for it."

Bob says he sometimes feels guilty about accepting gifts from Al. Bob is not the kind of guy to go around doling out gifts like Al does.

According to Bob the greatest gift Al has given him is nothing you can wrap in a box.

"I have met a lot of other people as a result of knowing him."

Maida Barron has known Al since 1993. She admires him because he places so much value on maintaining friendships over the decades.

"He's very loyal to his friends. They are still committed, loving friends. It's amazing. They know he has been there for them. He is very generous. He is very thoughtful."

Maida knows Al can be cantankerous, but he is dependable.

"There were many years when there was tough sledding for me. I could always count on him for laughter and that is very important."

Geoff Hanks said, "Al genuinely cares for human beings, period. He adores his daughters. He is not bashful about telling people how much he cares about them. He has become such a part of my life. I met him just after my grandfather had died. There was a kind of void left and Al helped me fill some of the gap left there. He's one of my best friends. His age doesn't come into my mind. It's just two people talking. I tell people one of my drinking buddies is an eighty-two-year-old man."

Jim Bradlin is the owner of James Clothiers. The store features exquisite men's fashions. Jim grew up in Beachwood and got his start in the clothing business at the Burkhardt-Davidson store at Severance Center in Cleveland Heights. It had replaced the Harry Jacobsen's store there. Al has been a loyal customer of Jim's ever since he opened his own store in 1980.

Jim said, "There's a handful of specialty stores that exist in this market. We all seem to develop a niche. I think my niche, rather than serving men under fifty, is serving men over fifty. That's my reason for still existing. The support of customers like Al Gray is the reason we have lasted thirty years. Without that loyal support, we wouldn't exist."

Al not only buys clothing for himself at James Clothiers, but he regularly purchases gift certificates there and hands them out to his friends.

Jim remembers how generous Al was when his friend Alan Schonberg turned seventy.

"I have never had a customer as benevolent as what he did for Alan Schonberg."

Jim likes to take credit for allowing Al the opportunity to dress up over the last three decades, but he is aware Al has a tendency to dress down as well.

"That's probably part of his demeanor. As I always say, you can't have a front without a back. You can't have love without sorrow. Sometimes you can't look good without looking bad. I fall into the same category as Al. Al and I have the ability to look like a homeless person, and then look like we are the king of the ball."

Al's friends may joke about his occasional fashion missteps, but Jim knows Al's classy side as well.

"Al has a great sense of fashion and appreciation for color and style. He is open to looking at things. He is always fun. He has always been pre-emptive. He would see something in a magazine and want to get it, or duplicate it. I would find out who made it and bring it in for him if I could."

Bold looks are just part of Al's fabric.

"I think it helps keep him young. He seems to be able to transcend the decades. New fashions appeal to him. Al doesn't have to admit to being over fifty, because he doesn't act it."

Arlene Fine's husband Phil said Al is the most generous man he has ever met. When Jerry Seinfeld came to Cleveland for a performance at Playhouse Square, Al Gray made it a special evening.

Arlene said, "He bought thirty-two tickets. First, he took everyone out to Chinese food. He called ahead to a restaurant and had all the food set out on platters. I didn't know all the people on his guest list that night. I never saw such a conglomeration. I'm not sure Al even knew all of the people who were in the group."

Al can rub some people the wrong way. There can be squabbles or standoffs. "No Seinfeld for you" may be a resulting consequence.

But Arlene says Al usually comes around.

"Once you are a friend, you are a friend. Even if you had a falling out, he comes back. He doesn't like to lose a friend. He's very loyal that way. So you can have a disagreement over a used car or a bad deal, unless you really did something horrible, he'll call you back in six months and invite you for dinner."

Why has Al been able to hold on to friendships that date back to his childhood? Geoff Hanks has a couple of theories.

"Good people are hard to come by. Maybe his friends know too much about him. They would make terrible enemies."

Arlene has known Al for fifteen years and values his friendship deeply.

"Those of us lucky enough to be in his world, can only smile when we think of him. Certainly he has his foibles. He's human. He's an eccentric millionaire. His compulsive buying is not routine behavior. Yet as much as he buys himself, he gives so much to others."

Why are people drawn to Al Gray?

Arlene said, "He's so convivial. He is the original raconteur. He's the last of that generation. He's a character times ten. You don't meet people like him too often, and that's his attraction. You never know what the next game he's going to be playing, what adventure he's going to get into next."

Marriage

Anita Belsito grew up in Cleveland's Kinsman neighborhood. She was the daughter of Peter and Mary Belsito. Anita was raised Catholic, but went to public schools. She graduated from South High and married soon after graduating. That marriage would not last long.

Anita began working at Management Recruiters International. It was a company launched by Al's long-time buddy Alan Schonberg. Al did a lot of the company's outside legal work. He and Anita began a courtship.

They would marry in 1975. Al was forty-seven. Anita was twenty-seven. Al's decades as a bachelor were over.

Anita said, "Here was this bon vivant, and I fell in love with him."

Al said, "In many respects, marriage was the greatest thing that could have happened."

Alan Schonberg was thrilled he brought Al and Anita together.

"They were very happy and very devoted to each other."

Al Gray's bachelor years were very busy with his work as a lawyer. He also spent much of his time doing all he could for his mother, Lottie.

51

Al's sister-in-law Ruth Gray said, "He was very good to his mother."

Al's mother returned the affection.

Ruth said, "We would be at a family gathering. Al was single and working long hours as a lawyer. His mother would always say, 'Let's wait for Al. Let's save that for Al.' She wanted to make sure the best part of the meal was left for him. Once we had prime rib, and she made sure to save some for him. She went overboard for him. She catered to his every wish."

But now, at age forty-seven, the most important woman in Al's life was his wife Anita. The marriage got off to a great start.

Anita said. "I think we had this idyllic life until he got sick. It was terrific. He was a great, great, human being. It was a learning experience for me because he was very sophisticated and I was not. He was in many ways, a great mentor. It was a great relationship."

Anita's parents were immigrants from Sicily. They embraced Al.

"He can come down to anyone's level. He could talk to average people, or to a king or a President. He can relate to people at all different strata of life. My parents loved him. They were very happy. They saw I was happy. He was kind and loving to my parents."

Al has been deeply committed to Judaism, but has maintained an open outlook about marrying outside the faith.

"I have a lot of respect for inter-marriage because I have seen a lot of good ones come out of it. If I were more Orthodox, perhaps I would have a modified view of it. I am a comfortably adjusted Jewish person who has liked being Jewish. Many young families adhere to Jewish-ness if one of the spouses is Jewish. It's a comfortable religion which accepts liberality."

Anita made the decision to convert to Judaism.

Four years after their wedding, Al and Anita had their first child. When Lottie was born, Anita was thirty-one and Al was fifty-one. Rachel was born three years later. The family settled into a home near the Oakwood Country Club in Cleveland Heights.

Al said, "It was a wonderful neighborhood. You felt good about how you lived."

Oakwood was a Jewish country club.

"It was built by Jewish immigrants who couldn't join country clubs that had restrictions or limits on Jews."

Al knew all about restrictions. John D. Rockefeller's Forest Hill development in Cleveland Heights and East Cleveland had deed restrictions that prohibited selling homes to Jews. The Van Sweringen brothers who developed Shaker Heights blocked Jews from that community as well.

"Those restrictions were awful. They were crushed in 1946 when the U.S. Supreme Court ruled them unconstitutional."

The Gray family moved to Shaker Heights in 1985. Al bought a home on Parkland Drive. It was right across from the Duck Pond, one of the Shaker Lakes. He paid nearly half a million dollars for the house.

Al relished the role of being a father. He didn't want to miss a minute of it. He made the decision to ease himself out of his law practice so he could devote much of his time to his young family. He introduced his daughters to international travel. They accompanied him to Israel fourteen times.

The divorce was tough on everyone.

Rachel said, "Divorce is an adjustment for everybody anyway. Couple that with the experience of him being in the hospital already, I think we were all learning about the new family structure. Immediately after the hospital stay, my parents wanted a fifty-fifty split of the kids. So I remember going back and forth to their houses. I was still young enough that I thought it was kind of fun. I do remember him being unstable at times, when he got out. Occasionally behaving in ways I knew wasn't normal. I knew I had to deal with it. I don't remember thinking less of him, or thinking anything negative. I remember thinking he's my dad. I love him. He's got problems, but he's my dad and I love him."

The divorce settlement would drag on and on. Soon after things were settled in November 1992, Anita began a relationship with Abraham

Feldesman. They would be a couple for fifteen years until his death in 2008. Al was taken aback at their relationship at first. He started dragging his feet in terms of fulfilling his obligations under the divorce. Al and Anita retained lawyers and the discussions got contentious. The bickering lasted three years.

Anita couldn't take it any longer.

She said, "I realized I don't want to do this any more. I just made the decision, he didn't have to do anything. My attorney went up to him and told him it's over, saying Al didn't have to fulfill his obligations to me. Al was outraged. He said I can't do that. From that moment on, things changed. It got better."

Through it all, Anita said she kept things as private as she could.

"I never said anything bad about him. I went to my friends, and I went to his friends, and said I hope you will support him, and you will be his friend too. And when you give that kind of blessing, it's much easier for people to deal with. It's not, who shall I like?"

She was able to continue to respect Al.

"I have so much admiration for him. He has come back from mental illness. We saw it. We saw it up close and personal. When you are mentally ill, it's not like you have a cancer or a broken leg. It's very scary, and most people don't know how to deal with it. He is blessed with a very strong emotional and physical constitution. He was always a man of courage and convictions."

The page had been turned. There was no going back for Anita. Getting back together with Al was out of the question.

"The breach in trust was so bad. I love this man, and I will love him forever because he's a pretty incredible human being. But I could never resume the marriage part of it. I couldn't. My big worry at the time he was ill, was he was going to shoot me, shoot the kids and then shoot himself. For a long time, I would go to bed at night not knowing if I would wake up the next morning. Where was I going to go? The man had enough money to find me if I took them and ran, so I decided just to stay here and roll the dice. There's a trust element. I can be his friend.

I can be his helpmate. I can be a lot of things to Al, but I can't be his wife. It was years of abuse. It took an awful toll. It doesn't mean I don't still love him, cause I do."

Anita and Al had been through a lot. The mental health setback was rough on both of them. The resulting threats from Al were frightening. The divorce was painful, but Anita said she was determined to learn from her struggles.

"You learn who your friends are. You learn who you are, and who you are not. You learn shit happens. There's nothing that can happen, that I don't know how to handle. You learn you are a survivor, and learn you are going to stay standing in a room because you've been through all of this. It gives me the confidence that I wouldn't have had otherwise. It was a freeing experience. It freed me of all the bullshit in life."

Early Law Career

W hen Al finished law school, and passed the Bar, he would have probably liked the opportunity to join a decent-sized law firm. But his grades in the first year of law school were sub-par. He knew that would hurt his chances.

"The first year, I didn't take it seriously enough. My grades were moderate to poor. One D, the rest Cs. I just wasn't into studying that year. I was indecisive about law, and probably at that time, my dad's problems were coming home to roost."

Al's father's moving business was falling apart. His gambling problems were worsening. His parent's marriage was strained. Al and his parents lived in a one-room apartment. Al was reduced to sleeping in the living room on a roll-away cot.

"I think sleeping on the cot was a good thing. The guys who had it good their whole lives don't understand it. Who had money? I was on the GI Bill."

Camping out on the cot wasn't intolerable.

"I had just come out of the Navy, where I slept on a bunk. I had the use of my dad's car. My mother's cooking wasn't bad at all."

Living with mom and dad cramped his style to a degree. Did his girlfriends grumble about the cot?

"The one woman I entertained on that cot thought it was great, because my parents were away for the weekend. I had to find women who lived alone. Motel rooms also were available back then for two dollars."

After wrapping up his fairly disastrous first year in law school, Al took a job working in the shipping department of a company called Lampl Fashion at E. 24th and Superior.

"I worked at night and realized at that point, law school wasn't so bad after all. Shipping out clothing wasn't a way for me to work myself up in the world. That experience gave me renewed vigor for the second year of law school."

Al knuckled down.

"I thought the professors at Western Reserve Law School were good, to outstanding. They were all bright. They weren't all good teachers. Some were better than others."

His work steadily improved.

"My grade-point average moved up sharply, but it was still below B. Potential employers looked at things like that."

His law school buddy Ed Gold had just interviewed with a lawyer named Al Nozik. Gold wasn't interested in taking the job, but he recommended that Al give Nozik a call.

Al said, "He seemed like a good fit for me. He offered me an opportunity to learn."

Al Gray joined Al Nozik's law practice in 1951. He was located on the eighth floor of the Citizens Building at E.9th and Euclid.

"He had started me at 100 dollars a month, plus all the business I could bring in. A few months later, he gave me a raise of ten dollars a month."

Al Nozik wasn't a cookie-cutter lawyer. He didn't sit around waiting for personal injury cases. He branched out into buying land and building houses. He started in Euclid and then expanded into Lake County.

"In 1952, I helped him acquire the land which made him a millionaire. We negotiated with the B&O Railroad which had gone through bankruptcy. He had a deal where he took control of the property, but didn't have to pay the railroad until he sold each parcel of the land. It was a huge amount of land, the Mentor Lagoons. It gave him a lot of flexibility. He offered me to stay with him when he moved out to Mentor."

The property was hundreds of acres. Back in the days when the railroads were being built, they had cut deals with municipalities and gained control of large swaths of the adjacent land.

Al Nozik developed Mapledale Avenue in Wickliffe. He built eleven homes on that street in the early '50s. The homes were priced at $12,000. Buyers could get one by putting one hundred dollars down. The monthly payment would be one hundred dollars and that included property tax and insurance. Al Gray went out to Mapledale on weekends and dealt with prospective buyers.

"When the final home was sold, I brought Nozik my bill for $200 a house. A total of $2200."

Nozik asked, "Are you sure?"

"You told me to give you a fair billing and that's what I did."

Nozik cringed at the idea of shelling out $2200 to his young protégé for his house-selling efforts. He told Al he would go ahead and pay him the money, but from that point on, he would no longer be paid a salary. He would only be paid for cases he drummed up.

"I said knowing how successful you are, and how hard I worked for you, I thought it was a fair arrangement. I became unhappy with our relationship."

Al decided to part ways with Nozik. He rented out office space in the same building.

Nozik said, "Hate to lose ya."

Al said Nozik had scared off at least a half-dozen young lawyers who had worked for him before Al did. Al didn't regret his time with Nozik.

"It was a good way to begin my law career and I'm glad I did it that way. I was eager to soak up experience. I was a good learner. He was a teacher. He was a smart man. He was brilliant."

Al stayed in touch with his first boss over the years. They had a mutual respect for one and other, and as the years went by, their friendship rekindled.

"I spoke at his funeral, at his wife's invitation. She said I knew him as well as anyone. I called him a misunderstood visionary. I was among all of those who couldn't understand him. We assumed he was a lot more supportive of other people. That was not one of his strong suits to support others."

Al Nozik had a reputation of clashing with municipalities over his landholdings. He was a maverick. Many disliked him and his actions.

Al Gray was proud of his friendship with Al Nozik. Their office association had ended many years before, but in the eulogy, Al pointed out that Nozik was a man with many achievements. He enjoyed tremendous success and had a wonderful marriage to his wife Eleanor. Many only knew Al Nozik's combative side. Al Gray understood his mentor's gruff nature.

"He was like that because of his upbringing. He had a Depression-era mentality. He grew up in a non-Jewish neighborhood and he felt somewhat oppressed. When he was in elementary school, someone called him a name that was insulting to Jews. That's where his problems could have started.

"I trusted him. He was direct about a lot of things. He couldn't handle the topic of money very well when it came to paying people like me, but he was great on deals of houses and everything else. I think fairness is important. He had a sense of desperation that went with that era."

Al said he learned a lot in those Nozik years.

"To be as openly honest with people as you can be. The degree of honesty and integrity I brought to my life, paid dividends, and conversely, things I have done wrong, have caused penalties. My battle with mental illness was punctuated with untruths and misconduct. It equipped me to better understand myself and everything around me. I am a much better guy than I would have been."

Al doesn't think he had the greatest legal mind, but he strove to keep things together.

"I stayed focused. Law practice demands that you can't do a job as a lawyer without being extremely focused. The most difficult task was telling a person in a criminal case that they would probably wind up in jail. Or after meeting with a doctor, telling a spouse their loved one wouldn't be coming out of the hospital."

Al says in the early days of his career, insurance companies were more inclined to settle with policyholders. They would buy peace far more readily.

"It was rare when an insurance company didn't offer something to settle a case. Insurance companies are no longer flexible like they used to be. I used to have a field day with insurance companies. I knew all of the claim adjusters and claim managers. The companies found out later that they were giving away too much money to lawyers like me."

Gray's Law

Al remained in the Citizens Building for the first ten years of his career, but then set up shop in the Superior Building near Superior and E.9th. He was a general practice attorney.

"I was a pretty good trial lawyer. I earned good fees and was very successful. I got good results for my clients. I wasn't a big-time lawyer, getting million-dollar verdicts, but I got respectable amounts of money for my clients."

Al was very dedicated to his craft. He put in long hours. He worked very hard. He never minded that. He always wanted to do the best for his clients. He thought working as a lawyer was a lot of fun.

"The emotional aspect of divorce cases was tough. I did all sorts of legal work, but I think the practice of divorce law is best done by guys who only do divorce. If you are not immune from the emotion, it's painful to see what goes on. You've got feelings for the people. You know the people."

There were plenty of reasons people sought divorces. A husband or wife was caught cheating. One spouse was spending too much money. A wife was not willing to have sex often enough. A husband wasn't paying enough attention to the kids.

"I turned down cases of some people I knew, but tried to be helpful to them in other ways. I knew some of their frailties, and I was able to help them overcome them. I had some great successes. There were those who were on the verge, who stayed together, and rebuilt their marriages."

It was an era when people didn't get divorced as a quickly as they do now. Al says in many divorce cases, honesty is hard to come by.

"You found people lying to you. That's a hard thing to overcome. You didn't get a fair shake on truth. They hide an affair. Hide a forgery. Hide a form of misconduct. I learned a lot of what to avoid in marriage, and how to deal with the conflicts that developed."

Staying together can be a challenge. Exercising good judgment is critical. Al knows controlling emotions is vital. He says his divorce from Anita was in large measure, because of emotions that got out of hand.

"I think in the divorce cases I handled, most of the cheating was for emotional reasons rather than physical. Sometimes the physical needs were satisfied at home, but the emotions were lacking. There may have not been an initial physical attraction with someone they met, but it led to sex impulsively."

Straying from a marriage was less common decades ago, but Al thinks birth control made it easier for many to have more sexually active lives.

"When marriage vows were broken, the impulse was to go to court and demand a lot of money to make up for the wrongdoing. One of the reasons that the divorce process can be easier today is that people are prepared to think less of the emotion, and a little more of the money, which enables them to just put it on a more business-like basis and makes things easier."

People can become disenchanted in a marriage early on.

"The rabbi says you are married, and right away, they start looking for a divorce lawyer. I don't like to see so many divorces taking place now."

Al never thought it was right to collect his fee for handling a divorce and then divorce himself from the person he represented.

"I worked very hard with people after their divorces. My greatest pride was in the post-divorce atmosphere to help them get their lives straightened out. A lot of them were crushed by the divorce. That was a major part of my illness dealing with my divorce. My primary purpose in law was to help people have better lives."

Ask Al about the bad rap lawyers have earned and he says. "We've earned it."

Actually Al respects the world of law.

"I love law. I always did. I found it terribly challenging and sometimes overwhelming, but wonderful, exciting. You are helping a person. You are helping all of society. In terms of a democratic country, you are helping the entire country to be a better place, if you practice law in an appropriate way. Even if your role as a person, may be minor in the scheme of things, you can set a pace for other people."

As a partner in his law practice, Bob Luria saw firsthand what made Al a good lawyer.

"He had a talent of making his clients like him and trust him. He had a good work ethic. He worked long hours. He had good relationships with his clients. He had a strong desire to do a good job for them."

Bob Luria started working for Al in 1966. He was paid fifty dollars a week.

"A lawyer who was a friend of my dad's, knew Al, and mentioned me, and Al was looking for someone. He let the other lawyers in the firm do what we wanted to do, but he kept his eye on everything. He always wanted to be kept current on what was going on."

Bob said Al was a master at handling personal injury cases.

"He had a good rapport with not only his clients but with the adjusters as well. That was a lot more important in those days, cause now the insurance companies don't pay anything. Back then, it was a different scenario. Al was also very good at business law."

Al says he has encouraged dozens, perhaps hundreds of young men and women to enter the legal profession. He says good lawyers are always ready for battle.

Al brought Keith Belkin into his law firm in 1976.

Keith said, "I learned a lot from him. He was good at what he did. He was a good people person. He related well to judges, juries and clients. In those early days, he would tell me things about life, and now that I am older, I understand what he was telling me. He taught me how to be a lawyer. He taught me how to relate to people and taught me my way around the courtroom."

Al said, "When you are across the table from somebody, he may have been your best friend, but he's not your best friend when you are on opposite sides. It may help in your negotiations, because you know how to communicate well, but you have to remember he has an opposing viewpoint."

Al's law career has proved useful in all sorts of business dealings.

"I use my legal background a lot. Not to file suits. I negotiate in my head the best way to handle a situation."

Jim Bradlin has gained a lot of respect for Al over the course of their thirty-year friendship.

"I think Al is a very good negotiator. I think you become a good negotiator when you are fair. If you are not fair, you are not a good negotiator because eventually, you won't complete any deals."

Jim knew Al was interested in buying a home on Parkland Drive in Shaker Heights. The owner was a one of Jim's customers at James Clothiers. The owner had poured a ton of money into the home to make it a real showplace. It was unlikely he would recover all of that investment when he sold the home to Al Gray.

Jim said, "That purchase was a real Al Gray coup."

Jim thinks Al has mastered the skill of hammering out deals that allow both parties to walk away with a sense of accomplishment.

"I think he looks for what he wants, and sees if he can create the situation that is favorable for both parties. That's what makes his negotiations successful."

Al's accountant David Polk knows what was the driving force behind Al's work as a lawyer.

"I think to be successful at the level he was successful, your major desire has to be wanting to help people. He gives back."

It's not a good idea to cross Al Gray.

Al said, "I am not going to stand still for mistreatment. I think one of the most important things in life is to develop a value system that allows you to judge where you are. You can still be wrong a lot of the time, but your values often steer you in the right direction. Maintaining your values is a constant challenge. There are temptations of every type."

Gary Simson, the former dean of the Case Western Reserve Law School, said he can picture just how effective Al must have been as a lawyer.

"I would find it hard to imagine he ever lost a case. He's such a perceptive guy. I'm sure he'd be incredibly savvy, and know strategy. He must have been terrific. He could interview a person, and in five minutes, tell if he is getting it straight or not. He's a good judge of people, and I think that would make him a good lawyer."

Al agrees that sizing-up people is vital.

"A skill I developed in my law practice was making judgments about people, as to who was telling me the truth, and who was not. This was not only in criminal cases but in civil cases where there was also a lot at stake."

Bob Luria recalls that working with Al provided many benefits, but there were some rough spots too.

"He was pretty easy to get along with, although he did some things that were excruciatingly annoying. Just after I got married, he had us work on Saturday mornings, which my wife hated. Around twelve o'clock, he would go into his office with a client and say, 'Hang around, there was one thing I wanted to talk to you about, as soon as I am done.' At two o'clock, I'd still be sitting there, waiting for him to get done, and he'd finally get done and he'd come to me and say, 'Are you still here?'

"You told me to wait."

"Oh, it can wait 'til Monday."

Al admits he was a taskmaster to some degree, but he was acting in the best interests of the law firm.

"We all had different outlooks on what was important. When an office is open five-and-a-half days a week, those were our hours. For all three lawyers not to be there on Saturday morning during that era, was unheard of. I would like to think overall, I was very fair-minded."

Bob said, "He would do the same thing during the week at six-thirty, or seven at night. That's why I say he was not that considerate of what was going on in other people's lives. He did that to everybody. He had to be totally in control. That's him. Total control. He was definitely a control freak. I resented him for that. Definitely. I don't know what makes people want to be controlling like that. Sometimes, he was a little shortsighted about the employee's needs."

Working as Al's accountant had some challenges as well.

David Polk said, "I used to walk on eggshells in the very beginning as our relationship developed professionally. I was always candid with him, but I felt I had to watch my words, so as to not possibly offend him. In our relationship now, that's not the case. I am very comfortable in saying what I want, no matter how it comes out. It's like dealing with a parent. There are times you can't be quiet and you have to say something. You need to not be afraid to speak up and stand up for yourself, but at the same time, have some humility and know when to say, okay I hear you."

David says he realizes everyone is unique. People have their quirks. He always adapts to his client's needs. What has David learned from Al?

"There's not only one way to look at things, and everyone has their own perspective. Al is very opinionated, and at the same time, he'll respect what you have to say. He'll modify what he is saying at the end with, 'Okay, I hear you. I understand.'"

Organized Chaos

If a police officer stepped into Al Gray's expansive home, he might wonder if the thieves got what they were looking for. The home looks like it has been ransacked. It is loaded with all sorts of fascinating treasures, but your eyes are first drawn to the heaps of items scattered everywhere. There is hardly a bit of free space on any table or countertop.

Al's home is by no means dirty. It's just surprisingly cluttered and jam-packed with letters, random photographs, old magazines and newspaper articles that Al has ripped from one of the three newspapers he reads every day.

Anita said, "He's a packrat. He's got a wild range of diverse interests. He is the most diverse person I know, and those interests all gather things. After the divorce, when he got on his own, that's when it took off."

A large poster board stands propped up against a cabinet. It's from Al's eightieth birthday celebration, a year and a half ago. Well-wishers scrawled birthday greetings on it. The fact it still remains on display is to a degree understandable. In a nearby room, yet another poster board leans against a display case. It's from his daughter Rachel's Bat Mitzvah, some fifteen years ago.

Harold Mendes said, "It's chaos. It's unbelievable. He throws everything on the floor. The UPS guy knows his place better than any other house in Moreland Hills. There's stuff arriving there all the time. He buys six of something, then he starts giving them away."

Al employs a cleaning lady. In fact, he has a couple of them. If they were to actually put every single thing away, they would stay busy for a decade or so. Incredibly, Al has a handle on where most of his belongings are stashed. Give him a moment or two, and he can lead you to a particular item. Often it is buried under a couple of oversized books he has just received from the Smithsonian.

Rachel said, "He bought this huge house. He didn't have enough to fill it up. So he started buying things and just never stopped."

Once you grow accustomed to the clutter, you realize there are indeed hundreds of treasures scattered around his home. There are Lalique glass figurines from France. Some are placed on shelves, others are inside the numerous display cases. So many items, large and small, it seems it would be impossible to look at them often enough to fully appreciate their beauty.

"That's why I live here," Al said.

One display case features a small glass emblazoned with a picture of child star Shirley Temple. Al doesn't remember how, or when he acquired it.

A few inches away, three baseball bats are next to each other, leaning against the wall. They are autographed by Johnny Mize, Stan Musial and Frank Thomas. Al didn't wait outside ballparks to get the bats autographed. He purchased them from dealers.

Several steps away, your eyes notice one of those pedal cars like boys used to ride in their neighborhoods in the '40s and '50s. This is no run-of-the-mill relic. It is fashioned to look like an Air Force jet. Al purchased it at a charity auction. It's a creation by famed artist and designer Victor Schrekengost. Al remembers paying $2200 for it. The pedal car is signed by Schrekengost.

A leaded-glass lamp of antique vintage sits on the floor next to the pedal car. Al says it isn't a Tiffany lamp.

On a shelf above, sits a collection of various figurines. Al says one of them is The Mendicant. It depicts a blind musician dressed in Middle Eastern garb. He says it's the first Royal Doulton piece he bought. It cost $28 and he got it while on a trip to Miami in 1952. Al says a similar piece these days carries a price tag of as much as $500.

His friend Alan Schonberg questioned, "Have you ever seen anything as abnormal as what his house looks like?"

Al's house has two sets of stairs to get to the second floor. When you reach the top of the back stairs, you come upon a jersey signed by Cleveland Browns Hall of Fame quarterback Otto Graham. It's not an old-fashioned jersey like the one Graham actually wore. Instead, it is the type of jersey you can buy now at a sporting goods store. Al had it upgraded with a custom-made Graham nameplate on the back. Many remember Graham's uniform number with the Browns was 14, but Al chose to have the number 60 placed on the jersey. That was the number Graham wore when he was with the Browns in the days the team was in the All-America Conference. Al had his daughter drive down to Mansfield to get the jersey signed when Graham was appearing at a public event.

Al points out a display case that features a collection of autographed baseballs. One of them is signed by Ralph Branca and Bobby Thomson. Branca coughed up the ball that was launched by Thomson in that one-game playoff at the end of the 1951 season. Thomson's "shot heard 'round the world," earned the Dodgers a trip to the World Series. This was not the actual baseball that changed history. But to have the signatures of both participants from that classic moment, on a single baseball, is indeed valuable. One of the players also scrawled the date 10/3/51 on the ball.

The display case also has balls signed by Jackie Robinson, Bob Lemon, Stan Musial and Ted Williams. A California Angels cap signed on the brim by Nolan Ryan rests on top of the baseball display case.

Nearby, sits a cigarette lighter. It was a gift from Al's parents sixty years ago when he graduated from law school.

A picture of Al's beloved Akita, Suzee Que 2 grabs your attention. Al decided to get an Akita after he saw a picture of the breed in a book.

"When she was two years old, she was diagnosed with autoimmune anemia. The vet said you will have her for six more weeks. Perhaps two months. She lived to age eleven. She collapsed and died when I was at the height of my mental illness."

Suzy Q 1 was Al's first dog. He named the dog after a World War II bomber. He got Suzy Q while a student at Cleveland Heights High. She was a cocker spaniel. While he was away in the Navy, Suzy Q was hit by a car and killed. Al's parents couldn't bring themselves to tell Al about the tragedy. They told him that the dog ran away. Many years later, Al learned that Suzy Q was killed.

A hallway features a painting of the Don CeSar Hotel in St. Petersburg, Florida. It was one of those grand hotels from the Great Gatsby era. It featured distinctive stonework that was pink in color. The "Pink Lady" had its grand opening in January 1928. The painting brings back fond memories of the days Al would take his family on vacation there.

Leaning up against a wall is a small oil-painting. Al says it was purchased in India in 1962 during his first trip around the world. It is the first work of foreign art he purchased. He paid about $50 for it.

Maida Barron has a strong professional background in art. Over the years, she has helped Al acquire works of art and furnishings for his home.

She said, "I have gotten him original pieces by major artists. I think he's got a really good visual eye. I think he loves color. He loves design. I think he gets very excited and turned on by the visual."

He points out a display that commemorates the time his daughter Lottie tried her hand at being a beautician. She was a pre-schooler, grabbed a pair of scissors, and trimmed the locks of her younger sister Rachel. There are a couple of pictures snapped a few minutes after the unauthorized event. To round out the presentation, some of the hair snipped by Lottie is under glass as well.

Not far away, is another framed exhibit that shows pictures of Al as a young boy. Some of his curly locks from his first haircut are preserved for all to see.

You come upon a shrine, of sorts, in a hallway. It honors Al's friend Wynell Schweitzer. The picture shows Wynell as a fashionably dressed woman with flowing blonde hair. Al says he spotted Wynell having lunch in a restaurant with one of her girlfriends. Al introduced himself and bluntly asked her if she would like to have lunch with him the next day.

She agreed to go out with him, and that was the beginning of a friendship.

Al said, "I think we responded to each other in a variety of ways. She liked to travel, so we did a lot of traveling. We just got along. She didn't call me every minute of every day to find out what I was doing. She was very supportive of me and I tried to be that way of her. For quite a while, it worked."

Alan Schonberg says Al and Wynell had a special relationship.

"She was a lovely, lovely, lovely person. She had the clothes, the jewelry, the minks and the cars. She was very attractive. She was smart as a whip. She was into culture. She was a great lady. She would not go out with Al if he was dressed like Bozo the Clown. If they went out, he would have to dress properly, and she even started to institute some sort of orderliness to his house. She was an extraordinary lady. Anyone who would meet her, be her in her company, would never forget her, and think very highly of her."

Arlene Fine said, "Of all of Al's girlfriends, Wynell was the best for him. She was flamboyant. She had blue mink coats and purple mink coats. Al and Wynell were so well-suited for each other. She liked to have a good time and so does he. She was six feet tall and even wore heels. Al is short, and here he was with someone who looked like a Vegas showgirl. She was like a party-girl. Al could close a party, even at his age."

Geoff Hanks was impressed by Wynell.

"She was a great woman. The way I would describe her is 1940s class. Just class. She walked into a room and it was elegance. She was just the definition of elegance. I have never met anyone like that."

Rachel Gray said, "I don't think they were same, but they complemented each other very well. She was very good at keeping him in line. She would come over and help him with his paperwork. When they would travel, she would come over and help him pack."

Al said, "Wynell was very patient. She was a terrific dresser. An attractive woman. She always wanted to look good, sound good, and act good."

Sadly, Al's relationship with Wynell would come to a tragic end.

Al said, "Some years earlier, Wynell's husband had taken his own life. He had some sort of cancer. They were members of a Suicide Society. Wynell was burdened with these incessant headaches. She couldn't deal with them any more. She didn't tell me what she was going to do. She killed herself, four years after her husband took his life."

Wynell had talked about taking her life someday.

Al said, "I didn't agree with her outlook, but I didn't want to stop seeing her because of that outlook. After a while, I realized I wasn't going to change her mind. At word of her death, my first reaction was horror. She had done what she had talked about doing and she had done it on her own will. The fact I didn't agree with her and didn't want to see her do that, didn't change the fact that was her way of dealing with life."

Wynell had helped Al acquire art objects for his home. She got Al interested in opera. They often attended concerts. She was definitely eye-catching, often wearing one of her sixteen fur coats. The coats were mink or lynx.

Arlene said Wynell was one of the few people who could make headway in the mess inside Al's home.

"She kept him on track. She would come in before parties and clean up the place. We had a couple of fundraisers there and I remember appealing to her. I asked her what we were going to do. People are coming in two days. She reassured me, saying she would take of it. She brought in boxes and put all the papers in them and got the place ship-shape."

Besides the large picture of Wynell, her shrine includes a doll that was hers. It sits on a small chair she had owned. There is a decorative wastebasket and a couple of other items that belonged to Wynell.

You can tell Al misses Wynell. She had traveled with him on trips to Europe and to Israel.

Arlene said, "She was wearing six inch heels as they walked on the cobblestones in Israel. I think Al liked the fact an attractive woman like Wynell was attracted to him."

Wynell kept her home in pristine condition. A stark contrast to Al's. She had a vast collection of china figurines. She grew roses in her garden. Many of the flowers were purple, her favorite color.

Arlene said, "She was eccentric, and he's eccentric. That was a perfect match. Their eccentricities matched each other. They didn't clash. They understood that part of each other."

Geoff Hanks said, "You looked at her at seventy-six and said she was still gorgeous."

Wynell was perfection in so many ways. Rachel thinks she had difficulty dealing with the fact that it was becoming more and more of a challenge to stay perfect as she got older.

"She didn't want herself not to be that way. Maybe that's why she killed herself. It was a combination of her mental state, this, that, and the other. She didn't want to be something else than how she wanted to be perceived."

Wynell had gone to specialists about her headaches. Nothing worked. Al recommended she go to a psychiatrist. She refused.

Rachel said. "I had just seen her a day or two before she died. She was very kind, even to strangers. She was very kind to everybody. Even with her strong opinions and views, she was always very kind."

Geoff said, "She valued your viewpoints, and even if it was different from hers, she would value what you said to her. It would spark a discussion."

Rachel said, "I knew about the decline in her mental state. No one thinks that someone is actually going to do that."

Across from the Wynell's shrine, is a print featuring the skyline of Cleveland. It was created by Peter Max. It is adorned by his signature.

Further down the hallway, there are a couple of framed tributes to Cleveland Indians Napoleon Lajoie and Tris Speaker. Each features autographs of the players. Napoleon Lajoie joined the Indians in 1902 and a few years later, was named player-manager for the team. He was such a prominent figure in Cleveland, the team was called the Naps for a few years.

Several pages from the Heights High *Black and Gold* and the Roxboro *Rocket* are under glass on the hallway wall. They feature sports columns written by Al when he served on the newspaper staff at the schools.

There's a bedroom that is used for storage. A picture of Al, Lottie and Bill Clinton hangs on the wall. This is the room Al uses to keep some of the many items he buys on sale. He stashes them so he can have them on hand to give as gifts to friends.

Al's bedroom has a silver statue depicting David slaying Goliath. They stand on a large block of stone. He says it is a work by famed Israeli artist Yaacov Heller. He says the piece was given to President Gerald Ford by Israeli Prime Minister Yitzhak Rabin. It wound up going back to the artist, who then sold it to Al.

Next to that is a Guardian of Zion award. It was presented to Al by Fuchs Mizrachi School in Cleveland. Al has provided support to the school. He is impressed that the school makes a point of sending its students to Israel for visits.

Al has a closet adjoining his bedroom. That closet is the size of a small bedroom. You see an array of colorful shirts. They are not subdued. The colors are bold, bordering on garish. Al is not afraid to be noticed. His prized shirt features outer-space moons and planets. Al says he picked up that shirt while sailing on the Queen Elizabeth 2.

Maida Barron says his flair for the outrageous has served him well.

"I think that has been what has kept him going, the fact that he has been able to be gregarious, outgoing, and exploratory. He is interested in the entirety of the world. He loves learning about new things."

Al explains he once traveled to England aboard one of the Concorde jets. He says flying at 1300 miles per hour was a thrill, but says the Concorde was not a very economical aircraft.

He points out a picture with his dad, his six uncles. Al begins identify each of them. He starts reciting each name, then mentions that person is no longer alive. Then he stops for a second, realizing of course, all of the relatives have passed on quite some time ago.

Walking back to the hallway, he points to a picture that shows clouds resembling huge puffs of cotton.

There's a picture that shows Al and his daughter Lottie standing in front of a helicopter. They had just taken a flight into the Grand Canyon.

There is a print on the wall that shows Cleveland Stadium. Just before it was torn down, Clevelanders were given the opportunity to take one last look around.

"I drove down there, but just couldn't bring myself to walk inside. I sat inside my car for a while and then drove home."

Al spots a Life magazine from 1939. He had another copy of this particular issue at one time, but lost it. He paid $25 to get this replacement. Al wanted it because the magazine featured a detailed description of the ships in the British Navy. As a young boy, Al was fascinated with the military. The cover of the magazine has a picture of The Deutschland, a German warship. It was one of the commerce raiders used in the early days of the war to attack British merchant marine supply ships.

Al remembers a similar German ship, the Admiral Graf Spee, which was called a pocket battleship. It was the size of a cruiser, but it was armed like a battleship. The crew had sunk nine merchant marine ships. The goal was to try to disrupt the flow of supplies to the Allies. The Graf Spee was surrounded by three British ships, and sustained heavy damage. The captain chose to scuttle the ship in Montevideo, Uruguay. It was given up to the sea, since it was unlikely the crippled vessel could make it back to Germany. Three days after sinking his own ship, the captain of the Graf Spee killed himself. Al's recall of World War II events is stunning.

The dining room table would be a featured piece in most other homes. At Al's you hardly notice that it's there. If Al were to host a dinner party, it would take hours to clear the clutter off the table, and put everything away somewhere. He picks up a Fitch Report from 1950. It was the information sheet he relied on when he purchased his first stocks. He then holds up the confirmation sheet from his acquisition of those shares of Royal Dutch Petroleum. The sheet indicates this purchase was for five shares, for a total of $163. Al maintains that he had placed these documents on the table to show them to me. I can't be sure, however, that they haven't been sitting out in public view for more than half a century.

When looking at them now, what does Al think about his life as an investor?

"I'm a lucky guy."

A nearby showcase features two of the three fossilized dinosaur eggs Al owns. He says they are certified to be 100 million years old. He bought these two from a store near the airport in Baltimore. Another egg is displayed near the front entrance. He got that one in England about twenty years ago.

Al is extremely proud of a moon rock he has. His buddies at the Air and Space Museum in Washington had presented it to him as a gift in recognition of his continuing support. There is also a picture of Al at the museum. He is surrounded by officials and several astronauts. They are presenting him with a wristwatch. That watch had actually been taken to the moon on one of the missions.

Al said, "It worked better on the moon than it works on Earth. You have to wind it 250 times a day to keep it going."

Why do the folks at the museum choose to honor Al like this?

"They like me."

Al's daughter Rachel and her boyfriend lived with Al for a year and a half.

Rachel said, "Geoff told me, living with Al Gray, it's the only place in the world where I have to move a piece of the moon in order to make a piece of toast in the morning. A piece of moon rock was sitting on the toaster."

Geoff said, "The first time my family came to the house, they said it must be amazing living here. I said it was amazing until you go looking for a pair of scissors. In the year and a half I lived here, I don't think I ever saw the same thing twice."

The same showcase has a picture autographed by President James Garfield. There are pictures of Al's ancestors from the old country. Seemingly out of place is a large plastic jar of petroleum jelly. It appears to be thirty or forty years old. Al encourages me to look closely at the label. It was sold by Gray Drug, the chain run by his Uncle Hy.

There is a 3x5 white note card that has an autograph of World War II hero Jimmy Doolittle. A few steps away, there is more extensive tribute to Doolittle. It features a cover of the book *Thirty Seconds over Tokyo*. There is a letter written and signed by Doolittle. It was a response to someone who had inquired about his courageous bombing run on Japan in April of 1942.

Doolittle wrote, "In answer to your question, we had a job to do, and did it to the best of our ability."

Doolittle downplayed his pivotal role, but Al speaks highly of his strategic attack on Japan.

"Roosevelt thought unless they did something in a hurry, American morale was going to continue to go down. So they came up with a plan to have the planes take off from an aircraft carrier and hit military targets in Japan. Shipyards, airfields and naval installations. It had a negative effect on the Japanese."

Sixteen B-25 bombers were used in the raid. After the bombs dropped, the pilots couldn't fly back to the aircraft carriers because the planes were too large to land on them. They had to crash-land the planes. Some pilots wound up in China and were assisted by people there. The Japanese military went to great lengths to discourage the Chinese people from helping American pilots again. They got their message across by massacring 250,000 civilians during the Zhejiang-Jiangxi campaign.

Three pilots were killed when their planes crashed during that initial attack on Japan. Eight crewmen were captured by the Japanese. Three were executed by firing squad. Another died in captivity following starvation and torture. Four remained prisoners of war and were freed by American troops in August 1945.

Walking up the front staircase of Al's home, you are dazzled by an entire wall painted with dinosaurs. Al had commissioned an artist to paint the original mural while Al was living in an apartment on Van Aken. He had the artist not only move the huge painting to his home, but had him expand it as well. The wall is accented by four ceramic figures of dinosaurs. Each is about the size of a small cat. Al came across them in a store in New York and just had to have them.

"They had them in the window. I'm crazy about dinosaurs. Why wouldn't I want to buy them?"

Al thought the dinosaurs in the original mural appeared too calm. For the expanded version, he requested the artist to include a more ferocious beast.

"When I was a little boy, I liked a few things intensely. Mickey Mouse, electric trains, and the dinosaur era."

As we continue our journey through the house, Al says few homes are large enough to adequately display such a huge collection of unusual items.

"There is so much wall room."

At the top of the front stairway, there is a photograph of Winston Churchill, Franklin Roosevelt, and Joseph Stalin. It was taken at the Potsdam Conference.

"I'm a big fan of Churchill. You'll find Churchill stuff all around the house. He was one of the greats. He took over the British government in 1940. Churchill roused the British people to supreme efforts to protect the nation."

Al points out that the early radar systems helped England defend itself against German bombers.

"Radar would tell them when German planes were coming over the Channel. They knew where they were headed, and knew the approximate speed. This allowed the British pilots to go to their planes only when they knew the bombers were on their way. They didn't have to be in the air constantly. It saved the Western democracies."

A dinner plate with the image of Winston Churchill is displayed. It commemorates the fortieth anniversary of the Battle of Britain.

There is a huge, ornate table imported from France. Al's baby gown sits neatly folded on that table.

"My mother kept the baby gown. I didn't see it until after she died. She wasn't one to display things. I'm the one to display things."

The table from France has detailed metal ornamentations. An invitation to Al's Bar Mitzvah is displayed. It was February 15, 1941. The ceremony was at Tacoma Shul. The reception was on Silsby, in the house his parents were renting.

How did Al do at his Bar Mitzvah?

"Everyone thought I did spectacularly, especially the people I paid to say that."

Ceramic figures of Moses, Joshua and Ruth are placed on the French table as well. A stone relief on the wall above, depicts the Exodus from Egypt.

A distinctive, colorful prayer shawl, or tallis, is displayed in a plastic frame on the wall. Al decides to backtrack to show me a chair that sits at the top of the stairs opposite his dinosaur wall.

He explains that was his mother's favorite chair. It was in the library of his apartment on Van Aken. His mother would sit in the chair and watch television during her final years. She was battling breast cancer.

"She let the problem go for a year. She had it. She knew she had it, but was afraid to own up to it. Like it was going to go away. She told me about it at breakfast one day. We had the opportunity to keep her happy for so long. She was comfortable. I had a couple of women who would care for her. She was a very kind, gentle woman."

The wall alongside the main stairway is covered with so many items, you nearly fail to notice two large paintings. One is of Washington crossing the Delaware. The other portrays the signing of the Declaration of Independence. Nearby is a photograph of Abraham Lincoln. He is visiting the battlefront during the Civil War. Another display features a note and autograph from the President.

"I got that in France. I went to an art house, and there it was."

Lincoln wrote the note on December 8, 1863. It was when he proclaimed amnesty for those who initially supported the Confederacy, but who were then willing to take an oath pledging their support for the union.

A glass table sits at the entryway to his home. The base is a huge carving of an Egyptian Pharaoh. Al displays some Royal Doulton mugs on the table. There is one for British Prime Minister Neville Chamberlain. One for Roosevelt, Stalin, and Churchill. Al boasts that the Churchill mug was named Mug of the Year for 2009.

A frame holds a picture of Rachmaninoff hovering over a piano. There was an autograph on a separate slip of paper encased in the same picture frame. But the years have been unkind. The signature has faded completely. At first, Al couldn't remember who the man was in this picture. I took the frame off the wall and found the name Rachmaninoff printed out.

Sergei Rachmaninoff was born in Russia in 1873. He was one of the leading composers and pianists of his time. He spent much of his later years in the United States. He suffered with Marfan syndrome.

That caused his fingers to be especially long. That helped his skills as a pianist. It may have also helped his handwriting. But since his autograph has faded away, Al can't verify that.

A frame holds not only a picture of Antarctic explorer Admiral Richard Byrd, but a check he wrote to Mary Byrd in 1933. The check is for ten dollars. No need to try to cash it now. It was cashed and appropriately cancelled by the bank. Byrd had deep American roots. He was able to trace his Virginia ancestry back to John Rolfe, and Rolfe's wife Pochahontas.

Speaking of members of the tribe, Al proudly displays a baseball autographed by Dodger left-hander Sandy Koufax. A Koufax baseball card sits nearby in an elaborate glass holder.

There are signatures of Thomas Jefferson, Andrew Jackson, and John Jay.

There is a letter to Al from President Gerald Ford. Al had written to the President in 1974 to complain about remarks made by General George S. Brown. Brown was chairman of Joint Chiefs of Staff at the time.

The general caused a stir when he told a reporter that Israel was becoming a burden to the Pentagon. He maintained that the United States continued military aid to Israel because Jews in America controlled the banks, the newspapers, and politicians.

Brown said, "They own, you know, the banks in the country. The newspapers. Just look at where the Jewish money is."

Ford apologized for Brown's remarks in his letter to Al Gray. The President reprimanded Brown and urged him to resign. Brown did not.

A large horse, forged out of brass, stands in a corner. It is probably more than one hundred years old. Someone along the way has added paint in pastel colors for accent. Al purchased it during a house sale at a mansion.

A small shelf alongside the steps to the basement is adorned with four *Alice in Wonderland* figures. They have good detail and appear to be rather delicate. Al says he bought them at a store near Walt Disney World.

A porcelain statue about eighteen inches tall, stands on a pedestal. It brings back plenty of memories for Al. It was acquired by Al's father during his house-moving career.

"We used to kid him about things he would filch from the job. The family joke was, 'Dad, didn't the people you were moving, miss it when you took it?' Filch was a term used in the '20s. When he saw something he really liked, he'd say to the people, I'll knock something off the bill if you give me this."

Al says his father didn't grow up with the arts, but he always had an appreciation for artwork that featured nice-looking women. He says his father's primary vice was gambling. A secondary one was grabbing an occasional figurine or vase.

Right by Al's front door is a basketball signed with a thick Magic Marker by seven or eight members of the Cleveland Cavaliers. It is difficult to make out the names. A Browns helmet is easier to discern. It has signatures from Otto Graham, Jim Brown, Dante "glue fingers" Lavelli, Paul Warfield, Lou Groza, Leroy Kelly and Bobby Mitchell.

There is a Joe Gordon model baseball glove. A Joe Jackson glove. "Shoeless" Joe Jackson was a country boy who got caught up in the Black Sox scandal of 1919. Players took bribes to throw the World Series.

"He went his whole life without being able to sign his name. Finally, toward the end, they taught him how to sign his name."

Al says the lamp that features two women fashioned out of porcelain, is perhaps one hundred years old. It sits on a marble pedestal. He says the lamp was his father's. He isn't sure if his dad purchased it, or he borrowed it from a customer.

A showcase outside of the library, features ancient artifacts. Most were unearthed in Israel. They are thousands of years old. There are candle holders, a baby bath fashioned out of marble, and glass perfume bottles. He has a rather large water jug that is believed to be three thousand years old. It stands near a weathered, yet intriguing gargoyle that was once part of a building in Europe. Al bought it in Florence, Italy.

One work of art dominates a section of the living room. It's a sculpture fashioned by artist John Clague in Cleveland in the '30s. It has bold lines. It was forged out of steel. When you apply pressure to the base, the sculpture rocks back and forth. That causes some welded balls to strike blades of steel. A symphony of sorts ensues for a minute or so.

Al says Clague was an art student when he constructed this. It took him three years. Clague sold it for $3800. When the woman who purchased it died, her son didn't have room for it. Clague bought it back for the original price. Clague was looking for someone to give it a new home. Al shelled out $3800 for it.

"I got the greatest piece in the whole world at its original price. I decided it was for Al Gray. John Clague wanted it to be in good hands. Someone who would respect it."

The artist was so concerned about the musical sculpture, he would come by Al's house from time to time to make sure it was in good tune.

There are four dazzling pieces of stone seated on Al's mantle piece. There is a rare flat piece of decorative glass created by Lalique. There are numerous Hanukkah menorahs among all the treasures.

There is a long, curved black couch. Not far away, is a couple of black living room chairs. They are accented by a couple of swans. What appears to be the elongated necks of the swans form an eye-catching border for the chairs. Their heads are on the armrests.

Al spotted the chairs in the window of a shop in New York. He was met inside by the creator of the artistic chairs. He says she was a statuesque blonde woman. She was dressed formally in a long, flowing dress. She explained to Al, she would have to handcraft a couple of new chairs for him. She told him it would take six to eight weeks for her to complete the project.

Al left a hefty deposit for the chairs and for some other pieces of furniture.

"Her husband ran the business-end of the enterprise. We paid fifty percent of what the cost was to be. Soon after, the husband made off with the bookkeeper, and took all of her money. One-hundred-seventy-five-thousand dollars. The artist was broke. It took her two years to get the chairs delivered here."

Al's library has a poster from Al's all-time favorite movie, *Citizen Kane.* There is a shelf occupied by the books he read to his daughters when they were young. It's a collection of Dr. Seuss books. There are small statues of Abraham, George Washington and Christopher Columbus. There is an exquisite flower vase that belonged to his mother.

He points to a figurine of a woman that stands about eight inches tall.

"This is the first piece I bought my mother when I was in the Navy. It was for Mother's Day in 1946. It was made by Royal Doulton."

The library houses most of his cherished Winston Churchill items. There is a letter signed by baseball Hall of Famer Rogers Hornsby. A dramatic statue of a man and a woman. Al bought that in 1955 on a visit to New Orleans. A classic grandfather clock made by Herschede.

The nickel tour of Al's treasures has taken more than three hours. It makes one wonder what plans he might have for all of this.

"I had an idea a couple of years ago. I called an art dealer who does auctions. We talked about giving half of the proceeds to charity, and the other half to my daughters. But I wondered why I would be in such a hurry. Someday, I would like to have my daughters retain exactly what they would like, but their interests are not precisely mine. I have a great appreciation for all of these things. I enjoy being home. I really don't get bored here. I like what it means to live in this house."

Lottie has this outlook.

"He is eighty-one years old. He has earned the right to do whatever he wants with it. He enjoys looking at certain things, at certain times. He'll buy something even if he doesn't have any place to put it. Some of those pieces are so individual and unique it's hard for people to appreciate them when they are surrounded by thirty other pieces on the wall."

Some might criticize Al for being so self-indulgent, but Rachel doesn't.

"He's got the money to do what he wants. He gives so much to so many people. It's not like he keeps all of his money to buy these things. If he wants to live this way, who am I to tell him not to? How can we not respect what he wants to do?"

Rachel says she has straightened things out in the house many times, but somehow overnight, it's just a mess again.

"He gets up early in the morning. It's too early to call anyone on the phone, so he just starts rummaging around. He goes into the garage. He goes through boxes and brings things in the house. That's how he discovers all these things."

Rachel thinks her dad's house, crammed with relics, and his closet jammed with outlandish shirts, are both just part of his fabric.

"I guess that's just his thing. He goes all-out in every aspect of his life. The clothing, the house. It's just part of his personality."

On occasion, all of the clutter can have a direct impact on Al's lifestyle. He is the proud owner of a four-door Lexus, and a sporty two-door Mercedes. It's not a bad idea for Al to have a back up. Shortly after Thanksgiving 2009, Al misplaced the remote-entry key to the Mercedes. It was somewhere in his house. The problem was, he had sometime previous, also misplaced the second set of keys. The Mercedes was parked in the garage. Al couldn't use it.

"Briefly, the loss of the key bothered me. I had to go to the dealer to order a new key, but if that's the worst problem I face, I'm not in bad shape. My daughters are not in trouble, my son-in-law is not in trouble. My former wife is not in trouble, so what problems do I really have?"

Al was by no means thrilled with the inconvenience of all of this.

"Last night, I spent an hour an a half going through my closets looking for the key. Today I instructed my two housekeepers to really keep an eye out for it. Nothing. Zero."

So Al drove the Lexus over to the Bedford Auto Mile to get another key for the Mercedes. The Mercedes dealer doesn't hand out these keys like candy. First, the replacement keys cost $205.65 each. Al ordered one, hoping one of the two missing ones will eventually turn up. Secondly, the replacement key had to be ordered in person, and it has to be shipped directly to the dealer from Texas. Al will have to make a second trip to the dealer to get the replacement.

If Al is fired up to continue searching for the original two sets of keys, he may come upon keys from the first car he ever bought. It was a 1955 Pontiac. It was a luxury model with leather seats. It was two-toned. Al paid $2800 for it. He got it at a dealer on Euclid Avenue. Replacement keys for that car probably cost thirty-nine cents.

City of Champions

Cleveland, the city of champions. It sounds ridiculous just to say it. A sizeable percentage of Clevelanders have absolutely no experience relishing in the achievement of a championship. But in 1948, Al Gray was among those who took great joy in celebrating Cleveland winning not just one championship, but three. The Indians, Browns and Barons won it all.

Al said, "At the end of the 1948 regular season, the Indians won a one-game playoff to get to the World Series. That was the greatest thing ever. They had a lottery to buy tickets, and I got three sets of tickets. I sold the tickets for two games, and kept the third set for myself. I got hundreds of dollars for the tickets I sold. I sold them right outside the ticket booth at the Stadium where I picked them up. I was debating keeping the tickets for those two games, but when I saw how much they were going for, I took the money. I could use it. I was just finishing undergraduate school at Reserve."

Al was in the stands for the Saturday game of the '48 World Series. Steve Gromek pitched for the Indians. It was the first World Series in Cleveland in twenty-eight years. Al couldn't believe all of the cheering, noise, and excitement in the ballpark that day.

"Larry Doby hit a homerun that day. It was a big thing to have a black centerfielder. Nobody knew if he was going to be any good. They didn't know if team owner Bill Veeck had just signed Doby for publicity, or if he had skills as a ballplayer. Turns out he had tremendous skills."

Larry Doby was the first black ballplayer in the American League. The season before, Jackie Robinson broke baseball's color barrier by joining the Brooklyn Dodgers in the National League.

"Joe Gordon, Indians second baseman, welcomed Doby with a handshake. Not everyone was doing that in the clubhouse. Joe Gordon was already my favorite player, so I loved him just a little more for doing that."

Al was glad to see discrimination against blacks easing somewhat when Doby was signed, but admits most fans hadn't dwelled on the issue back then.

"I didn't think much about it. It was assumed to be that way. Even if you were a freedom-loving guy, as I think I was, you didn't think that much about it, because there were not African Americans in my classroom, or in my neighborhood. So what was the big deal they were not in the Major Leagues."

Al has been waiting more than sixty years now for the Indians to win another World Series.

"I'm a patient guy."

He holds memories of 1948 close to his heart.

"With three teams winning championships, it made the city so spectacularly positive. It was wonderful."

Al saw his first Indians game in 1936 at League Park. He was eight years old.

"If there were any bigger fans than me, I don't know who they were."

League Park was at E.65th and Lexington.

"It had a high outfield wall in right field that extended from the foul line to the center field bleachers. The bleachers were small. Left field was just one deck. You were close to the field. I saw Bob Feller pitch the last game of the season. My favorite player that year was Earl Averill. He hit more than .400 for most of the year."

In 1937, Al went to the second game of the season. Then on Memorial Day he went to a doubleheader at the new Cleveland Stadium.

"It was one of the great, exciting moments of my young life. It was pre-television days, so the only way you would see a ballpark was in a picture in the newspaper. I liked the Stadium better than League Park. You are a nine-year-old kid. It was big."

Al followed baseball like he was team statistician.

"I was always big on numbers. You would know the averages. I would always know Earl Averill's average and know how many games Bob Feller had won. I would never be bored as a pre-teen watching a sporting event. If a game dragged, you would never say that's boring game. You just loved being there. Fans were dressier back then. Men wore suits and ties. It was the style of the time. Very few women came to games."

Al was also a fan of the Cleveland Rams. They were the Cleveland entry in the National Football League. His favorite player was fullback Johnnie Drake. The style of football was far different back then. A single-wing formation was common. The ball was snapped to the fullback by the center. It wasn't hiked to the quarterback as it is today.

The Rams won the NFL championship in 1945, but it was a hollow victory. The team never really caught on with fans, and owner George Reeves decided to move the team to Los Angeles. The West Coast was about to start a post-war boom. Airline travel was improving.

Football fans were about to latch onto the Cleveland Browns. They were in the All-America Conference and led by football genius Paul Brown. The war had ended, and players were returning from the service. Otto Graham was the quarterback.

"His record and his team's record of never having a losing season, will tell you about Otto Graham. If he wasn't the best in history, he was close. He started out at Northwestern as a basketball player. He had skill in ball-handling that was so developed, he could flip a football fifty yards. It was really incredible. He was not very fast. His intelligence was high, and he knew how to handle a football. A superstar."

Al thinks Otto Graham as quarterback, and Paul Brown as coach, proved to be the best one-two combination this town has ever seen. He says Brown was a genius. A winner with great judgment. He thinks Brown assembled the smartest group of players ever in Cleveland.

"It's hard to compare one era to the next, so you don't know if Brown was better than Vince Lombardi. The Brown name still stands for excellence and success. He had a positive impact on our community because the Browns were winners. I was saddened a great deal when he was fired. He should have been allowed to stay on as general manager."

The Browns were in the championship game in 1950, the first year they moved up to the NFL. Al wanted to go to the game, but a friend of his was getting married that day. Fifty-nine years later, Al was able to recall the score. The Browns beat Los Angeles 30-28. They proved to the world they were good enough to be in the more prestigious league.

Al took in a lot of Indians games in 1948 as they moved toward a pennant. He landed a summer job as a playground supervisor at Waring Elementary at E.31st and Payne.

"It paid next to nothing, but there were not many jobs around. I played baseball with the kids and I lost twenty pounds that summer. I got my body back."

Being on the fringe of downtown, gave Al plenty of opportunity to see his beloved Indians that summer. He took in a couple of dozen games.

Gene Bearden was the surprise left-hander. He won twenty games. Feller won nineteen. Bob Lemon won twenty.

"Lou Boudreau was the player-manager. He was well-liked. A good guy. He smiled a lot. He was a heck of a shortstop. He and Joe Gordon were as great a double-play combination as you will ever see. Both of them were relatively slow-movers and didn't cover a lot of ground, but they were always in the right position for the groundballs. They knew the pitchers. They knew what the pitch was going to be, and knew where the ball would be coming."

Geoff Hanks says he has discussed the year of champions with Al many times.

"I really like history and I like sports history, too. Cleveland is important to Al. He could have gone anywhere he wanted to go, and he stayed here. The ice of Lake Erie kind of runs through his veins. He has always called this place home. Why leave when you are already home?"

Anti-Semitism

─ ⁂ ─

Back when Al was just about five years old, his family moved from a rental on DeSota Avenue in Cleveland Heights, to another rental on East Overlook.

"The first day, as I was walking down the street with a friend, this guy Larry Monroe, who was about seven or eight, came by, and said, 'This neighborhood is becoming all dirty Jews.' That was my first encounter with anything like that."

It was by no means, a warm welcome to his new neighborhood. Al remembers feeling awful. He later became friends with Larry Monroe, and would eventually bring up the insult to him. Monroe told him to forget about what he had said. He told Al he didn't know what he was saying back then.

Al remembers talking about anti-Jewish slurs with his parents. He says his mom and dad reflected on how sad it was that harmful things were said in our free country. They told Al to be careful, and try to avoid confrontations over insults when he possibly could.

"I tried to be respectful of people. My parents were very respectful of people."

When Al was in boot camp at the Navy's Great Lakes Training Center, he was in a room where a lively discussion got underway concerning religion. He told the others there that he was Jewish. They all admitted they had never met anyone who was Jewish.

"I knew I had to be a careful guy if the subject of religion came up. I learned it wasn't wise to shout out about religious things."

Al says some of the bad feelings about Jews eased somewhat after World War II. He says a lot of people felt sorry for Jews because of what had taken place in the death camps. But ill feelings are developed early in home environments, and those feelings are not easily overcome.

"The parents had prejudices that were exhibited daily, and those affect children as they grow up. Fortunately, here in America, we have a high percentage of people who want to be respectful to others."

Al thinks there is far less anti-Semitism now than when he was young.

"I learned early on in my life, there would be people in my life, I didn't like being in my life, but they were. You had to know who you were in the world. I think I was very fortunate in learning lessons early, and being sure I didn't forget them. I was taught how to handle acrimony. How to handle personal conflict. Go easy. Go slow. Go softly. Keep your mouth shut as much as possible."

Al's goal was to diffuse potentially explosive situations, but he spoke out when he thought he should.

In regards to the anti-Jewish feelings in the Middle East, "It's a tough part of the world to deal with. Just when it seems to be under control, we encounter the greatest dangers. I think there will be a Palestinian state in the coming decades, but getting there will be a tremendous challenge."

Al felt a great deal of sadness for the victims of the massacre at Ft. Hood in November 2009. He said, "The alleged shooter, Major Nidal Malik Hasan was responding to teachings that have no place in the American military or in society."

How did Hasan's brewing issues escape detection? How did his suspicious behavior not send up red flags?

"I was especially offended that it was someone who had risen to the ranks of an officer. To do what he did, was just incredible. I think it's obscene what he did. He's got a huge mental issue. We have to be more careful in our evaluation of military leadership, but I don't think it's more than an isolated incident."

Al knows it can be difficult to get a true reading of someone. He served on grievance panels for the Cuyahoga County Bar Association. Lawyers who were suspected of misconduct would come before the panels, hoping to escape the punishment of disbarment.

"You would see people in front of you who seemed to be 100% good, yet they had done something that was completely unethical and illegal. They had to know it when they did it. We have to work toward educating everybody, but some guys are going to fall through the cracks. A lawyer who steals a client's money has fallen through the cracks. We were pretty harsh, especially on repeat performers."

Gunning down defenseless fellow soldiers is of course, a far more shocking crime than a lawyer cheating a client, but Al says it is often difficult to find out what is going on in a person's mind before it's too late.

The Crusade for Soviet Jews

The great pride Al took in his Jewish heritage, was openly displayed during his deep and long-lasting commitment to the plight of the Soviet Jews. It was 1966 when he got involved in the struggle to gain freedom for the Jews there.

"I had always thought the Holocaust against the Jews would never have started if the Jewish community around the world had been more active when it began. The fears of the Depression were so great, the leadership did not grab hold of the problems in Europe. I felt even though I was only one person, I felt I should do my best on behalf of the Refuseniks."

Al went on a trip that included stops in Moscow, Leningrad, and Kiev. He visited Jews there and learned how they were not able to practice their religion.

"It was a trip that stoked my knowledge and my interest. They couldn't get the hell out of there. There were a couple of million people involved, and they had no organized Jewish life to speak of. The older ones, survivors of World War II, were just glad to be alive. The younger ones had no background in religion. They were just controlled. Every one was controlled there. Not just the Jews."

The people who applied for exit visas and were refused permission, were called Refuseniks.

"Most of them ended up in Siberia, having been sentenced there for applying to leave the country. They were told they were now going to be residents of Siberia for doing that. Others started having sit-down strikes in Red Square. They were not afraid. They were gutsy people. It took a lot of guts to stand up to the Soviet government."

If a mother or a father would apply to leave, their entire family would be banished to Siberia. Five thousand Jews were sent there.

"The ones sentenced were pretty much highly educated people who wanted to get the hell out of the country because they didn't like the way they were being treated. They had been treated poorly in their jobs. Denied promotions. They wanted to empower the lives of their children. They wanted their kids to grow up free. There were labor camps. The Russians were masters at those. The Jews would be transported and deposited in Siberia. Imagine the guts it took to apply for an exit visa, when you knew your next-door neighbor had been sent to Siberia because he had applied."

Anita said, "I had known about the oppression these people had lived under, but it wasn't until I actually went there, and saw them, and touched them, and felt them, that I got it. It hit me in the face, and I really became active. That trip changed my life. It moved me in new directions. Everything happens for a reason, and that trip made me a zealot. It made me understand the less-fortunate, whether they are here in a hunger line, or anywhere."

Al took part in demonstrations here in the United States. He met with congressmen and senators urging them to support Soviet Jews. Al attended high-level meetings at the White House.

In 1971, Al traveled to Brussels. He was among 700 activists gathered there to speak out about the situation. The event attracted 700 journalists from around the world. The movement was starting to get attention. It was at that point, the Soviets started bowing to pressure from the West. They began letting some Jews leave. In one year, the

U.S. government appropriated $41 million to boost resettlement efforts. Many of the first to leave, headed to Israel. Later on, many settled in the United States.

"The Soviets were a terrible regime, but they were subject to world opinion. Releasing Jews was inconsistent with how they operated, but they tried to do things politically that were smart. They gained political support from the West."

Al is proud of his efforts to reach out to the Jews trapped in Russia.

"I feel that was one of the more valuable things I did in my whole life. We got more than a million freed during the Soviet regime. I was a part of a team of people that did wonderful work."

Lottie said, "Rachel and I grew up knowing our parents were very active. Growing up in the household we did, gave us an understanding and the appreciation for standing up for people who need help, no matter who they are, or whatever the cause. People who can't speak for themselves. I don't think everyone is raised with that awareness. I have a great appreciation for it."

A reminder of Al's commitment is always close at hand. He still wears a metal wristband engraved with the name of Vladimir Slepak. Slepak was an engineer. He and his wife Masha applied to leave the Soviet Union in 1973. He took part in demonstrations. He was one of the most well-known Refuseniks in Moscow. Al visited with him at his apartment in Moscow. Slepak was later arrested and sent to Siberia for five years.

Why does Al think the Soviets zeroed in on Slepak?

"He was the spokesman. He was the bigmouth. He organized a sit-down strike in Red Square. That is tough thing for the Soviets to deal with. Slepak was a tough guy."

Vladimir Slepak was eventually released and settled in Israel. Al invited him to Cleveland to deliver a speech in 1999.

Al's wristband has many nicks and dings in it now, but he continues to wear it proudly.

"It's my way of showing support for causes. Not just for Soviet Jewry. It's part of my support for Israel, for the Jewish Federation in Cleveland, for the Jewish Community Center, as well for freedom for everyone."

Rachel said, "I remember growing up, both of my parents having great compassion for everyone. Not just Jews, but people on the street, too. They were constantly traveling around the world to help other people. It's all I knew. I know not everyone's parents did those kinds of things, but I knew it was the right thing to do because that's how we were raised, and I still feel that way today because of it."

In the fall of 2009, *Refusenik,* a movie about the Soviet Jews fight for freedom, was premiered at the Cedar-Lee Theater as part of the Jewish Film Festival. Al Gray was sure to attend.

"I was prouder than ever having been able to participate in the movement. I was very proud of America for standing up for inhabitants of a foreign country."

Al had of course met the leading Refuseniks, so seeing their story told on the big screen, had a big impact on him.

Natan Sharansky's battle to emigrate to Israel was the most celebrated story. The day after their wedding in 1974, Sharansky's wife Avital, was allowed to leave the Soviet Union and move to Israel. Sharansky promised to join her in six months. His fight would endure for twelve years. He was released in 1986. He was unable to see his wife for all that time.

Al said, "What they gave up for freedom was incredible, unbelievable and impossible, but they made it possible. I love Sharansky. He was one of the greatest guys I ever met. Maybe the greatest individual ever. He didn't have to be the world's greatest Jew in order to want the freedom to practice his religion in Israel. His struggle was a symbol to Russian Jews."

Some of the Refuseniks were not imprisoned or exiled to Siberia. They were tossed into mental institutions.

"They declared them of unsound mind because they expressed interest in leaving the country, they supported Judaism, and had strong feelings against the Soviet regime."

The movie depicts the valiant the struggle for freedom waged by the Soviet Jews. Somehow, for many people, the drama of their fight is fading from memory.

Al said, "It's not a history of a revolution. You hear about revolutions. You don't hear about freedom movements. This was a freedom movement. It ultimately freed more than a million people from the harshest regime in the modern world. You have to understand how severe the Communist rule was back then."

Al urges people to see *Refusenik.*

"It's a special experience to those people who were involved, or to anyone who touched it. It's wonderful. The movie is important to those who remember the struggle, those who participated in it, and to those who benefited from it."

Cleveland area congressman Charles Vanik was a leading crusader to use trade sanctions to pressure the Soviet Union to ease its grip on Soviet Jews, and let some leave the country. Al thinks Vanik was a "fabulous guy" who helped push the cause. He also credits Washington senator Henry "Scoop" Jackson. Together, they sponsored the Jackson-Vanik amendment.

Al said, "In some respects, I was sorry the era ended, because the results were so stunningly successful. The campaign to free Soviet Jews helped to break down the entire Soviet system."

During the height of the Cold War, it seemed unlikely the Soviet Union would collapse. Premier Nikita Khrushchev was such an imposing world figure.

Al said, "Khrushchev seemed to be representative of all Soviet leadership. He was smart enough to know when to bang his shoe on a table, and he knew how to handle the media. Most of the time, he did a good job of getting to the forefront of newspapers and television to get his point across about how good Communism was."

The beginning of the end of the Soviet regime may have begun in 1963. The Cuban Missile Crisis, the standoff between President John F. Kennedy and Khrushchev, is of course easily found in all of the history books. Kennedy applied pressure to get the Russians to remove missiles from the island of Cuba.

But in retrospect, the efforts of a handful of Cleveland men cannot be discounted. They were members of a small synagogue called Beth Israel - The West Temple. It was on the West Side of Cleveland, far removed from the Jewish stronghold of Cleveland's eastern suburbs.

Lou Rosenblum and Don Bogart were NASA engineers and members of The West Temple. In 1963, they were among the temple members who launched a group called the Cleveland Committee on Soviet Anti-Semitism. They were surprised to find none of the national Jewish organizations was looking into the probability that Jews in the Soviet Union were being repressed.

The movement they started gained momentum. A major springboard was a meeting held at Cleveland Heights High on March 7, 1965. More than two thousand people showed up for a rally that day. The success of the Cleveland group, led to pressure groups being formed across the nation in dozens of cities. A movement was born. The battle for the rights of Soviet Jews, was the first assault on the totalitarian regime in that country. The eventual destruction of the Berlin Wall was rooted in the outcry first raised in Cleveland.

Al takes tremendous pride in his activism on behalf of Soviet Jews.

"I went to the Soviet Union because I thought it was important individuals would be protected so they could have a better life. It was as pure a cause as you could have. If you live your whole life in a free society, you hate the idea of people living in less than such a condition anywhere in the world. I went there in part, because they were Jewish, but also because the Soviet Union was an enemy of the United States. Getting them to release Jews was part of it, but it also meant getting our government to deal with the Soviet Union as an enemy."

Joel Fox was director of social planning for the Cleveland Jewish Community Federation. He looks back fondly on his days working with Al Gray in his quest to free Soviet Jews.

"Al was a stalwart leader. Always at the head of the pack. Always ready to be supportive. Encouraging us to take people when other communities were kind of holding back. It was an expensive proposition. We had to resettle newcomers who were coming here with nothing."

It was a good deal easier for Soviet Jews to settle in America in cities where they already had relatives. Some Soviet Jews didn't have that opportunity.

"We took the largest number of people who were not related to people who were already here. They were called free cases. It was a very expensive decision for the community to make. Our leadership, Al Gray, Bob Goldberg and Albert Ratner felt very strongly that Cleveland, with a strong Jewish community, should take responsibility for the more desperate people. They saw it as an opportunity to build our Jewish Community."

Joel remembers that Al and Anita's home in Shaker Heights became an unofficial meeting place for planning meetings. The doors were always open.

"Among the Soviet Jews, Al was known as one of the Americans who cared the most, did the most, and was always available for any help or guidance. He had a depth of dedication in terms of getting it done. He just wouldn't let go, so when people would stand up and say, 'It's too expensive, we can't afford this,' Al would be one of the strong voices that would say, 'We'll find a way, it's is worth doing. I'll be generous myself, and I'll ask others to do the same.'"

Joel Fox says Al Gray was a source of inspiration.

"I found him to be an excellent partner to the professionals. He was a leader who was willing to do what he had to do. It was very satisfying and constructive to work with Al Gray."

To this day, Al feels a kinship with people who fled the Soviet Union. He has visited Europa restaurant at Lander Circle in Pepper Pike many times. On one occasion, he flagged down the owner, and engaged him in a conversation about his homeland.

Alex Shneyder is neatly dressed. He is fifty-six years old. Before launching Europa, he was the owner of a restaurant in Lyndhurst called the Russian Tea Room.

"That restaurant burned a year ago. The insurance money did not pay me enough to reopen it. I started looking for a place somewhere else. The owners of this restaurant had closed it down. It had the kitchen and the furniture. For forty-four years it had been called the Lion and the Lamb. After that it was a Mediterranean restaurant owned by a couple of doctors."

Alex has turned Europa into a place that serves hearty, home-cooked style dishes with a European flair. He then opened a Ceviche bar in a downstairs section of Europa.

"It features fish marinated in lime, lemon, or other citrus. New York City has more than four hundred Ceviche bars. They are popular in Peru and Ecuador."

Al Gray presses on, eager to find out more about Alex's background.

"Alex tells him, "My father was in the military. We moved all the time to different cities. The last place he was stationed was in Siberia, so that's where we stayed. I did not practice Judaism while growing up in Siberia. Where I lived, there was not one synagogue, none. In my city, there were ten thousand Jews. No one went to synagogue. Few people went to church there. There were only two or three churches."

Alex Shneyder eventually settled in Moscow to run a restaurant.

"Moscow is a great city, but when I was there, it was Communist. That's a problem."

Alex said he had relatives in Cleveland and they invited him to move here. He enrolled in an English class shortly after arriving in Cleveland. One of the other students in the class was a woman who had also settled in Cleveland after leaving Moscow. They wound up getting married. They now have two children and live in Pepper Pike, not far from Europa.

Alex explains he still closely tracks what goes on in Russia.

"Two days ago, a huge terrorist attack on a train between St. Petersburg and Moscow. Twenty-six people died. Everything is political. A huge bomb, two hundred pounds."

Al Gray shares stories with Alex about his visits to the Soviet Union, including the confrontations with the KGB. Most people in a restaurant would have just continued eating their scallops that day, but Al Gray will rarely pass up an opportunity to talk to someone. By reaching out, he made a new friend, and gained a respect for a man who has traveled halfway around the world to start a new life.

Stephen Hoffman, the president of the Jewish Community Federation says Al Gray's activism has changed many lives.

"Al has been an inspiration. When the Soviet Union was a dangerous, closed place, Al Gray went in without fear to contact people, to let them know they are not alone, that the Iron Curtain was permeable."

Joel Fox cherishes the time he worked on the Soviet Jewry resettlement with Al.

"I found it a privilege and a pleasure to be involved in that particular chapter with him because it did mean so much to him. Over coffee, or in a room with 500 people, talking to Al Gray, or listening to him speak about the needs of the cause, was very motivational to all of us."

The task was a daunting one. A Jew in Moscow or Leningrad wasn't just handed an airplane ticket and forgotten. Joel Fox says it was an overwhelming project.

"We needed day schools, the community center, family service, nursing homes, and Mt. Sinai Hospital to all work together for a package of educational and social services for the newcomers. Al was volunteer number one. It was an intense, difficult, expensive time. Al was always the first one at the table and very interested in the lives of those people. I loved working with him."

Al Gray as a toddler.

Al at age five.

Al and his favorite cousin Rita Gray.

Al's high school graduation
picture, 1945.

Al on the day of his Bar Mitzvah.

Al's parents Lottie and Rob Gray
on their thirty-fifth wedding
anniversary in 1951.

Al's brother Louis Gray,
his parents and Al.

Al Goldring, Irwin Gray, Morris Gray, Rob Gray, Joe Gray, Jerry
Agin. Hy Gray in back row.

Al's maternal grandparents, Bessie Weingarden and Joseph Weingarden.

Rachel, Anita, Lottie, and Al.

A trip to Paris. Rachel, Anita, Al and Lottie.

Lottie with her proud father.

Al, Lottie, and Rachel.   Lottie, Al, and Rachel.

Lottie and Rachel.

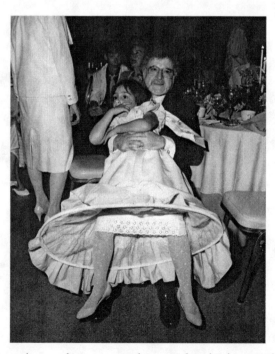

A night on the town and Lottie has had enough.

Case Western Law School reunion. Al in the middle. Fred Weisman is to his left. Ed Gold is further left, seated on arm of chair.

Rachel, Al, and Lottie along with an age-old friend.

Rachel, Lottie and Al.

The teenage years.

Al in Brussels in high style.

Al, Anita Friedman, and Al's psychiatrist, Dr. Ernest Friedman.

Al captured in a photo with President Barack Obama.

President of Israel Shimon Peres with Al.

Soviet Refusenik Natan Sharansky and Al.

Al, President Bill Clinton, and Geoff Hanks.

Al, in his legendary outer-space shirt, and Hillary Clinton.

Connie Schultz, U.S. Senator Sherrod Brown,
Lottie Gray, Hillary Clinton, Al.

Al and U.S. Senator Sherrod Brown in deep discussion.

Al in front of the Enola Gay.

Al with the pilot of the Enola Gay, Brig. Gen Paul Tibbets.

Wynell Schweitzer with Al on a visit to Europe.

At Smithsonian Air and Space Museum. Astronaut Tom Stafford on extreme left. Astronaut Gene Cernan on extreme right. Astronaut Wally Schirra, to the right of Cernan.

Lifelong friends Alan Schonberg and Harold Mendes join Al in his backyard.

Al posing next to his backyard totem pole.

A world traveler taken for a ride in Cambodia.

Al sits for a formal portrait.

Meg, William, and Eli Marger in front row.
Bernard and Al's niece Carol in back row.

Carol Gray with her husband Alan Gray, Al's cousin.

At age eighty, Al finally gets a chance to hold his first grandchild,
Azzizi Shalom Gray.

Getting down to Azzizi's level.

Al and Azzizi strike a pose.

Al, Rachel, Azzizi, and Geoff

A final time together. Rita Gray Newman, Al Gray, and Alan Gray.

Al, his law office partners, and their wives. Terri Luria, Bob Luria and
Betsy Belkin. Al, and Keith Belkin in back row.

Who Needs Anonymity?

Ruth Gray picks up the telephone in her apartment in St. Petersburg, Florida. She was married to Al Gray's brother Louis. Lou died nearly twenty-five years ago. His widow is now ninety. She is mentally sharp, and holds nothing back.

When asked to field a few questions about her brother-in-law, she says, "Am I supposed to praise Caesar, or something?"

Al's brother Louis was ten years older than him. When Al was a young boy, his teenaged brother was already spending most of his time in the Glenville neighborhood, courting Ruth Pollack.

Ruth reaches back seventy years to come up with this image of her eleven-year-old brother-in-law Al.

"He would sit there with these adult people and he was very sure of himself when they discussed politics, stocks, or statistics. He could rattle off a lot current events and was always sure of his facts."

She says even in his early years, Al opened his checkbook to causes he cared about.

"He does give to charities. He did that when he was young. My mother-in-law used to say Al belongs to the Audubon Society. I had a running joke that he was going to leave all of his money to the birds."

Al's good friend Harold Mendes has an ability to size up people. He knows Al as well as anyone.

"He loves attention. He does what he can to get publicity. I say to him, Al, I didn't see your picture in the *Jewish News* this week. What's going on? He has a big ego."

Arlene Fine is a reporter for the *Cleveland Jewish News*. She has written numerous articles about Al. You could almost say Al Gray is her newspaper beat.

"She said, "For a while there, there was actually a moratorium on Al Gray stories. At many events, he would sneak into the background of pictures. He loves publicity."

Al admits he loves to toot his own horn. He says there is nothing wrong with that.

"I don't think I ever wanted to be anonymous. Maybe I am excessively exuberant about not being anonymous."

Arlene says Al shouldn't be ignored by the newspaper.

"For the *Cavalcade* column, very often the pictures are taken at fundraisers, philanthropic events. He is so philanthropic. If an organization has a silent auction, he goes home with half the items. He will bid $3000 on a loge or on an airplane ticket. I've been there and I've seen it where he has written checks for $5000 or $6000. So, because of that, you want to honor the guy who has given so much. He loves his picture in the paper. So what does it hurt?"

To his credit, Al has an explanation about why he chooses to take credit for everything he does.

"We all like to be self-important. We want to set an example that other people will emulate. I believe I care about other people. Giving to charities is good for me, but more important, I think it's good for my children and my grandchild. It's good for the entire community that they can say, 'There's that guy, Al Gray, he does all he can, and he's helping.' We all like to be role models of some kind, and I think I can help to be a role model to some extent."

Al is proud he is trying to have an impact.

"A great deal of what I do is helping the world be a better place. I think that's my cause."

Lawyer Lee Kohrman, also a 1945 graduate of Cleveland Heights High, salutes Al for his involvement.

"I know he's very generous with the community. He is very responsible, and has been recognized for his generosity."

And that generosity has had a profound effect on others, inspiring them to get involved. Keith Belkin was a young lawyer working in Al's law firm.

"One day, he drove me home from the office, and I asked where he was going, and he said he was going to a nominating committee meeting. The organization was going to select the board of trustees. I told him he should put me on board, cause I want to start at the top. So he did, and that's what got me started."

Keith has since gotten deeply involved with many Jewish charities, the United Way, the Epilepsy Foundation and the Orange Schools Foundation.

"He got me involved in charitable organizations. He was the driving force that got me started. I always admired Al for his work with charities. That's one of the best things about him."

Sister-in-law Ruth Gray said, "When he does something, he likes to be noticed much more than the average person. He definitely likes attention."

The Case Western Reserve Law School named its rotunda after Al. The outdoor area at Fairmount Temple is called the Gray Garden.

Ruth said, "He likes his name on places, if a room or a wing is dedicated."

Al points out that it is actually the leadership of a temple or a school that decides if part of a building should be named in honor of a generous donor.

Ruth Gray gives Al a lot of credit for his accomplishments, and at age ninety, has earned the right to give him a jab, or two.

"He was a smart kid, really ahead of himself. He used what he knew to get ahead. It's admirable what he did, but a lot of people do it, and don't dedicate buildings to themselves."

But Gary Simson, of the Case Western Reserve Law School, says Al deserves recognition not only for his financial support, but for his unfailing enthusiasm as well.

"You don't get better supporters than Al. No school can make it without substantial financial support. Al has been incredibly generous. Because of Al, I think his friends are now more connected to the law school. He's really remarkable. He's sort of the model alum, in my view. People don't come any better. He really wants to help the school."

Geoff Hanks said, "At some point, you deserve recognition."

He says Al has lived in Cleveland all of his life. Over all the decades, he has come to know a large number of people. He likes maintaining connections.

"It can be a nightmare trying to leave Corky & Lenny's with him. He seems to know 500 people in there. It can take forty-five minutes to make it to the door."

Gerry Goldberg is chairman of Winslow Asset Management. He handles many of Al's investments and has keen insight into Al's civic involvement.

"He's a first-class person. His passion is people. A lot of people are involved in philanthropy or charitable work, some give their money, some give their time. Al gives both, but beyond that, what makes him different from other people is he also gives of himself in terms of a nurturing, and bringing in future leaders. He is so committed. He stays involved in the organization. Others may lose interest and move on to other things. Al keeps the commitments he makes. That's one of the most laudatory things about him. You can count on Al over an extended period of years. That's very, very unusual."

Bob Luria, who was a junior partner in Al's law firm, knows Al relishes being in the spotlight.

"I think he has had a major impact on the Jewish Community. He's a real philanthropist. Always has been. A lot of it is his ego. He's got a huge ego. Always has. Some people like the recognition. That's what they want. That's what success is to them. It isn't to me. We are nothing alike in that regard. Ego plays a major part in a lot of the things he does. I don't think anybody doesn't like him. I don't think some necessarily loved him, but they didn't dislike him."

Bob said Al never missed a chance to be the center of attention.

"People who need all of those accolades, want things for themselves like huge birthday parties, to have everybody there, making a fuss over them. That's the last thing in the world I would want. I have a hard time understanding why anyone needs to be in control of people, making sure people like you. I don't care if people like me or not. I don't have that need."

Bob and Al are in many ways, polar opposites, but Bob says to this day, the two of them get along just fine. He respects Al, and appreciates what he has done.

"He provided me with a living for years. He always made sure I was pretty much taken care of. When my wife and I were going to buy our first house, he made sure we had enough money. He gave me a raise when I needed it. He took care of me, pretty much. Almost like I was a son. I respect what he has achieved. He treated me well, but I still have some resentment for how he sometimes treated me, which was all about his control issues."

Bob says Al's need to be in control, still flares up from time to time.

"He still tries to be controlling today, when he needs something and wants something. 'I need a letter written. Did you get to that letter yet?' It's still one of his traits, wanting me to jump when he calls, which doesn't work so great anymore."

Keith Belkin doesn't fault Al Gray for wanting to bask in the glow of a spotlight.

"That's part of what makes Al, Al. That's what he likes to do. He likes to be in the limelight. It's part of his outgoing personality. It's good for him. You accept Al for who he is. If you know him, that's just who he is. Deep down inside, he's got a heart of gold."

Al's cousin Adam Fried says Al's charitable ways have rubbed off on a lot of people.

"He's been an inspiration. Whenever I am asked to give something to charity, I always think of him, and I reach into my pocket and do what I can. He's a very philanthropic person."

Al's friend Maida Barron says Al is a fascinating guy.

"He's incredibly bright. He's got a great sense of humor. He's got a steel trap for a mind. He remembers things. He can give you details on things."

But Maida knows Al can use that steel trap mind to remember details about himself.

She said, "He has a very strong sense of himself. He has a very strong ego. It doesn't matter to him what anyone else thinks, or anyone else says. Al's going to do what he wants to do. That's the way it is going to be. Most women can't handle that."

Gary Simson said Al really made him and his family feel at home when he moved to Cleveland to become dean of the law school.

"Of all of the graduates of the law school I met here, Al almost became an adoptive family member. Coming to a town you don't know, it's great to have people welcome you with open arms, and he certainly has. It really meant a lot. He's an upbeat person. He's kind of a cheerleader for people. He's a very forward-looking person. It is his ambition to be so helpful and move things forward in a positive direction."

An Olympic Tragedy

On September 5, 1972, Al Gray closely followed the terror in Munich, Germany. Eight members of a Palestinian terrorist group called Black September, had stormed into the apartments that housed members of the Israeli Olympic team. Two Israelis were killed shortly after the invasion, and nine others were taken hostage.

"I was saddened beyond belief that at that point in world history, such an event should take place," said Al.

Concern in Cleveland's Jewish community was especially strong. David Berger was among those seized. He was a graduate of Shaker Heights High. He spent his undergraduate days at Tulane, and then earned his law degree from Columbia University. He had moved to Israel. At age twenty-eight, David qualified for the Israeli Olympic team as a weightlifter.

David competed in those Munich Olympics on September 2, and was eliminated from competition.

The world was alarmed at the news of the Olympics being the setting for an act of terrorism. David's parents Benjamin and Dorothy anxiously awaited news about the safety of the hostages. They learned the terrorists had taken the hostages to an airfield. There was talk of transporting them out of Germany. Initial reports indicated the terrorists had been overpowered in a gun battle and the athletes were safe.

"They're all gone."

Those three words from ABC sportscaster Jim McKay turned a wave of optimism into pure despair.

David Berger had been in a helicopter at that airfield with three of his fellow athletes. The others were killed by gunfire. David was shot in his legs, but was still alive. One of the terrorist's detonated a hand grenade. A fire engulfed the chopper, and David died from smoke inhalation.

Three years later, a monument was erected at the Jewish Community Center at Mayfield and Taylor in Cleveland Heights. In 1980, Al Gray was president of the Jewish Community Center and took part in a ceremony as the sculpture was designated as a national monument.

Al said, "It was a sad occasion, but with respect for what he represented and what Israel represented. It was sad that people should die in that way."

Al got to know David Berger's parents.

"A tragedy of that magnitude, it's impossible for anyone to say they can deal with it. It's overwhelming."

The anguish over the loss of the Israeli athletes will endure, but the days of memorial at its original location were numbered.

The Jewish Community Center was opened in Cleveland Heights in 1960, but two decades later, there had been a population shift. There was a call for construction of a new JCC at a more centrally-located site.

"It was a challenge to find the right location. We weren't sure where to go. I headed up the team. The land we were interested in had to be rezoned. We worked with Beachwood Mayor Harvey Friedman. The negotiations took a good while."

The parcel in question was just west of I-271, between Shaker Boulevard and South Woodland Avenue. It was fifty-three acres.

"I thought it was great land. It was a lot of work. I could have been a full-time employee. We had more than 300 meetings. The land was rezoned and construction began. We had three million dollars for the construction. At first, we couldn't afford to build the auditorium."

The Beachwood JCC opened in 1985. Al gives a lot of credit to Mayor Friedman.

"I loved him. He was a nice, heavyweight guy in thinking and in weight. He was a good guy. Anyone who knew him over the years, had the utmost respect and admiration for him. He was a fine leader. He was a hard worker and wanted his community to grow and be successful."

In 2009, a controversy developed regarding a building in Beachwood, not far from the JCC. The headquarters of the Jewish Community Federation had been located at E. 18th and Euclid for half a century. There was a call to move the headquarters to an office building in Beachwood.

Al's friend, Bob Silverman has been a major force with the Jewish Community Federation. He didn't like the idea of a move.

"I was highly opposed to them moving to Beachwood. I thought it was insane, and I still do. They belong downtown. They have obligations and responsibilities to the city. It's the major headquarters of all of the other religions. They belong down there."

Bob said the Federation's board meetings were never very contentious. He thinks more healthy debate, especially about the transfer of the headquarters, would have been worthwhile.

"There weren't often differences. Maybe that was a problem. The problem with many corporations is members of the board often do nothing. The officers can get away with anything, and I think that is what happened with the Federation. Members of the board didn't do their responsible duties and they let the officers and executives persuade them to move. That's my opinion."

But populations shift. Demographics change. Building the Beachwood JCC was a major development. For more than twenty years, both the Cleveland Heights JCC and the Beachwood JCC remained opened, but the decision was made to close the Cleveland Heights facility. It was torn down and replaced with condominiums.

Al said, "I loved the old JCC. I hated to see them tear it down. I went back to that building and walked through it, but its time had come."

Jordan Rothkopf moved to Cleveland from New York City in 1979 to take a job as camping services director at the Mayfield Road JCC. He says Al Gray was president of the JCC at the time, and had played a role in hiring him.

Jordan said, "He was a very active president. In 1983 and 1984, Al played a major role in raising money for construction of the new JCC. As a fundraiser, he was superb. He knew how to ask, and knew how to tell the story of the JCC. He's very articulate. He was able to say why the JCC is so important. Why we needed to have a more convenient location. Why the JCC mattered in people's lives. His commitment was unflagging. It was a very demanding task, and we raised $13 million in a two year period."

Al had made his way to the leaders of the Jewish community back then. He explained his strategy.

"We were friends and respectful of each other's concerns and attitudes. They were all known to be generous givers to the Jewish community. I tried to get everyone involved, and I didn't do a bad job of getting everyone involved. We put up a first-class building for that era. I was proud of that building."

Jordan Rothkopf moved up in the ranks at the JCC as the years went on.

Al said. "I think Jordan has done a sensational job over the years, in what he does. He's one of the best people I have ever known. He's a good administrator and gets along with people. He knows what it takes. I'm very big on integrity. I would put that at the top of his list."

Jordan said Al took him under his wing at the JCC right from the outset. Jordan was a candidate to become executive director of the JCC in 1996. Someone else was selected.

"Al encouraged me to stay at the JCC after that disappointment. He was interested enough in me to tell me I was okay, and that I shouldn't leave to take another job elsewhere. I was very touched by that. It was at a time I felt rejected by the people I worked so hard for. He's been a warm person to me. He always wants to make things better. He wants to bring things to people. He's always involved in something, a cause or a person."

Al will oftentimes read about a need in the newspaper, or hear about a cause on a newscast. He will reach for his checkbook.

Al said, "Most recently, at Orange High School, there was something about the band taking a trip and they needed money. I often get involved with service organizations and veteran's groups. I grew up with that philosophy of helping those in need."

Jordan is impressed that Al Gray still makes the effort to keep in touch, even though Al's official role with JCC ended years ago.

Why did Al take such an active interest in Jordan's career at the JCC?

"I wanted to see Jordan succeed."

Al has always thought the JCC is important to not only members of the Jewish community, but to the overall community as well. He says members have to be involved with the vitality of the entire metro area.

The David Berger Memorial was not left behind at the site of the Mayfield Road JCC. It was uprooted and moved to the new JCC. It's forged out of steel, weighing 6,000 pounds. A fitting tribute to a young man who was a weightlifter. It features five Olympic rings. The rings are broken. The base consists of eleven pedestals. Each to remember the athletes and coaches who perished. It graces a peaceful setting. A reminder of a violent time.

Embracing Judaism

At the Jewish New Year service at Fairmount Temple in 2009, Al Gray was honored with a seat on the dais, and was called upon to read a prayer. There was a reception that Rosh Hashana outside in the Gray Garden. The temple built the garden after Al donated the funds for an endowment.

Al had been a member of The Temple - Tifereth Israel, for four decades. He stepped away after becoming disenchanted with Rabbi Ben Kamin.

Al said, "He was arrogant, and he was boastful about himself. He wasn't concerned enough with the issues of the congregation."

Al spent the next two years looking for a new temple. It was 1999 when he made the switch to Fairmount. He had always respected Rabbi Arthur Lelyveld, the former leader of that temple.

"He was outspoken. I had him speak at my mother's funeral in 1975. I was proud of his involvement in the civil rights movement. That's one of the reasons I went to Fairmount. I think clergymen should get involved in public issues."

Al's concerns about Tifereth Israel had been brewing for some time. He had issues there with Rabbi Dan Silver.

"I was in charge of community relations of the Jewish Community Federation, and he was in a sense, a subordinate to me. He was chairman of the Israeli Task Force. He didn't like being subordinate to Al Gray, or anyone else. His father was Rabbi Abba Hillel Silver and he thought he was a big shot because of that. He didn't like Al Gray."

On the other hand, Al had tremendous respect for Abba Hillel Silver.

"He was one of the big spokesmen during World War II. And after the war, he was a big supporter calling for the creation of the state of Israel. He was beloved and also highly respected in the gentile community. I admired his fire and power of speech. I found him gracious, humorous and a hell of an intellect. He had a powerful effect on me on the importance of Israel."

It was critical for Rabbi Silver to see a homeland developed for the Jewish people who survived the war. Al traveled to Israel for the first time in 1962.

"My feelings were stronger after I arrived. There was a change when I saw it, touched it, and was touched by the people."

Al says the next time he travels to Israel, it will be his fortieth trip there.

"There have been ups and downs with the government policies there, but my support has never wavered, either emotionally or financially, and it never will. But there are times I have been displeased with the policies depending on who wields the power."

To know of Al Gray's deep commitment to Israel and Jewish charities, you can only imagine his outrage and disgust at the actions of investment schemer Bernie Madoff.

"Madoff was terrible for the Jewish charities. He bankrupted many. He deserved all of the punishment he could get. Too bad there is no capital punishment for what he did. He was the worst. He was perhaps the biggest schemer in the history of the world. It was so awful. Stealing money that goes to orphans and little kids."

Al is a supporter of the American Technion Society in Haifa, Israel.

"It's a wonderful school and I have visited it. I got a call from them. They lost a fortune to Madoff."

Officials of American Technion said the school had initially placed $29 million with Madoff. It was told that investment had realized a gain of $43 million. The school therefore tallies its loss at $72 million. That represented a loss of 25% of its portfolio.

Before news of the Ponzi scheme surfaced, Al says he had never heard Madoff's name. He says Madoff's victims were smart people.

"Madoff's view was if you are going to be a crook, be a big-timer. Don't bother with little things. Don't bother with small bank accounts. But he didn't do it alone. He did it with a staff that was compliant. He was the most clever guy on the face of the Earth according to the people who gave him money. They had no direct reason to believe he was doing what he was doing. Their friends and neighbors were all investors. He didn't just take from strangers, he took from the people he knew."

Al hopes most charities can bounce back.

"Some charities will end up closing. Some will struggle and never regain strength. I'm going to help Technion regain its stature. The American Jewish Congress in New York is close to bankruptcy because of Madoff. I continue to send them some restorative money."

Al's financial support is nothing new.

"I was supportive of causes from the time I was a little boy. I made a contribution to the United Jewish Appeal after I learned of the death camps in Europe in 1942."

Rachel knows firsthand of the extent of her father's generosity. She helped him with his bookkeeping while she lived with him when she was in her early twenties.

"I saw essentially every check he wrote. My God, his charitable contributions every month, would exceed all of his other bills. He gives so much to so many people."

Anita says her years with Al taught her that helping others is the honorable thing to do.

"If somebody crosses your path with a problem, they came to you because you have the ability to help them. You have the ability to make that person's life better, and this is how I run my life. You just didn't come across this problem by happenstance. You came across it because you have the ability to help."

Lottie is proud of her father's involvement.

"A lot of people have the ability to help and choose not to. They don't get it. They have a different life philosophy."

Al's accountant David Polk says Al doesn't limit himself to merely writing checks.

"Just because someone gives hundreds of thousands of dollars away to organizations, with Al that's not the sum total. He's right down there in the trenches, trying to help people who might be down on their luck, or make some connections for them, or offer them advice."

Rachel says her father and mother have been an inspiration.

"Most people aren't able to take the time off to do those things. Most people don't see the importance either. Most people don't care, or most people write a check and that's it. It's incredible they were able to be involved in causes, and they still are."

Rabbi Yossi Marozov is leaving a meeting at the Jewish Community Center. Al Gray walks up to him.

"Al said let's go to the air show at Lost Nation Airport. I said okay. We get to his red Mercedes convertible and he says, okay you drive. As a rabbi, I am not used to driving a red convertible. I had a slight technical problem. I had a yarmulka on, and here I am driving sixty-five miles per hour. I had one hand on the steering wheel and one hand holding my yarmulka. People were driving by and thought it was very funny."

Al has known Rabbi Yossi for ten years. Al has provided money to support The Friendship Circle of Cleveland. It's a program that pairs up teenaged volunteers with special needs children. The volunteers make weekly home visits to their partners. The center in South Euclid holds carnivals and holiday events. Children take part in classes for dance, martial arts and improving their social skills.

"The children have all types of abilities, a range of abilities. We look to serve any parent who feels their child needs a friend."

Friendship Circle holds support groups for parents of special needs children and for siblings of special needs children. It sponsors winter camps and summer camps.

"Al Gray has always had a listening ear. He has offered financial support without me having to push."

Rabbi Yossi and Al have grown to be friends. The rabbi drops by Al's house and they talk about life values and about involvement in the Jewish community.

"Walking with Al Gray in the JCC, and seeing how he interacts with people, he always, always makes people feel good. Whether it's a little child, a mom holding a little baby, or it's just somebody in passing. Always a compliment. He will greet everybody with a smiling face or with a happy demeanor."

Rabbi Yossi has witnessed that people are often taken aback at Al's compliments. He says they stop and thank him and mention that they appreciate that type of compliment.

"I think he does this genuinely. He likes making people feel good. I see him do it, and I see how it works. It takes just a little bit of effort. It takes the time and a little bit of sensitivity to do that, but it certainly makes for happier people. He is a person who overextends himself to try to be everywhere. He loves life. I think a lot of it is natural. He has a tremendous appreciation for the beautiful values and the good life we have in America. There is no other Alvin Gray."

Maida Barron knows how devoted both Al and Anita have been to charities.

She said, "It's phenomenal. It's so important because the younger generation doesn't know how, or doesn't care. He sets a wonderful example. I hope the example he sets for his daughters will continue through for them. They have two amazing parents who are both very dedicated to the Jewish world. I hope that carries through for them and their children. They have had two of the most shining examples of Judaism, of what it means, what charity means, of what caring for others means."

Maida is concerned about the next generation.

"Our parents wanted us to be members of the greater community. To be assimilated. Our generation has kept that awareness of what it means to be Jewish and what it means to give back. I'm not sure the next generation is that aware, or that committed. It's unfortunate when you lose that awareness, you lose that need to protect your own, and be there for your own. You can be overwhelmed by the negative and that's very worrisome. Certainly, Al and Anita have set really strong standards."

Lottie says it is no coincidence she wound up in social work, helping those with mental health issues.

"I think my experience with my father's mental illness definitely steered me into my field. The way I was raised, the values I was raised with, definitely led to my involvement in the non-profit field. I became active in not only supporting the agency I work for, but other non-profits as well. I know the importance of being active in the community, and taking an active role in causes I care about. Using my gains to help others besides myself. Help those who are less fortunate. My dad taught me to try to be independent and better myself."

Anita says she is proud of Al. He has been a role model.

"He taught me the importance of staying standing. Not to let problems overcome you. The importance of being a survivor. A survivor of one of the most despicable diseases around, mental illness."

Al's cousin David Kottler is twenty years younger than Al. He says Al has inspired him to get active in social causes, and to support charities and people in need.

"He's very willing to lend a hand to people who probably aren't in any kind of capacity to ever repay."

Jim Bradlin said, "I think he is very focused on his philanthropy. He is civic-minded. He supports things that are dear to him."

Scott Fisher said it is not uncommon for Al to go on a buying binge for his friends.

"He once went into Border's and bought a huge number of books and just gave them away to his friends. That's the kind of thing that he does. I don't think he has ever turned anybody down who was trying to raise money for a worthwhile cause."

Al had served as treasurer of the Jewish Community Federation. With his track record of being president of the Jewish Community Center and president of the Jewish Vocational Service, there was a likelihood he would ascend to the board presidency of the Jewish Community Federation.

He said, "I had aspired to leadership roles, not necessarily titles, but leadership. In regards to the presidency of the Federation, would I have aspired to that? Not in terms of praying to God to make me president, but I felt if I continued to be a hard worker, a successful officer in the Federation family, others would have liked to see me succeed to the presidency."

Arlene Fine said, "If he hadn't had a bi-polar breakdown, he would have been board president of the Jewish Federation. It all fell apart. The fact that he is still friends with all of those guys, is amazing to me. That level of forgiveness."

Al said his mental issues were the cause of a number of setbacks. He doesn't think there was a chance to be named board president after his breakdown.

"I don't blame them for that. I don't think they could fully understand the consequences of my illness, other than to say, 'Gee whiz, can we trust him?' I was very, very sick. At the height of my problems, I had to be considered awfully sick. There was some percentage of chance it would have happened had I not become ill."

Stephen Hoffman, the president of the Cleveland Jewish Federation, said Al has been committed to serving Jewish agencies both on local and national levels.

Hoffman said, "Al has been extraordinarily generous with his time and his means. There aren't many Clevelanders who have served as effectively. He's a world-class Jewish personality."

Stephen Hoffman thinks there are four reasons Al Gray has been so devoted.

"Al's a lover of people. He hates injustice. He understands the need to look out for Jewish people because no one else will, and he's a mensch."

David Polk said, "When I think of Al, I think of a very philanthropic person. He has a heart of gold and an open heart to help everyone who crosses his path."

The American System

After passing the bar in 1951, Al wasted little time in getting involved in politics. He became chairman of a committee of lawyers supporting Tennessee Senator Estes Kefauver for President. Kefauver's efforts fell short. Illinois Senator Adlai Stevenson won the Democratic nomination.

"Kefauver was a liberal Democrat. I heard him speak in Cleveland, and I liked what he had to say about the role of the United States in the world, and what he thought we could do to improve things."

Al's involvement in politics has not wavered over the years. He went to a fundraiser for Barack Obama at the Renaissance Hotel.

"For me to shake hands with Obama, is a nice thing for me. I liked it. I was very impressed with the speech he made. Up until that point in the campaign, my favorite was Hillary Clinton. It probably took a couple of thousand dollars to go to the event. I was invited. I really did want to meet him because he seemed like such a viable candidate. Even at that point, I was continuing to support Hillary, but I wanted to know him better."

Al thinks President Obama inherited a real mess. He thinks he's off to a better start than a lot of people give him credit for.

"Bush's second term was very destructive to the federal government. I don't think he did a good job at all."

Al knows the new President has to contend with racism.

"We have a long history of racism. It's unfortunate, but it's there."

Al has hosted fundraisers at his home for a number of political candidates, including Governor Ted Strickland and U.S. Senator Sherrod Brown.

"I think it's healthier when people do get involved. I think letting it be purely party politics without people joining in, is bad. I have also contributed to Republican candidates. The Republican Party solicits me. I don't tie myself to one party. I have supported George Voinovich."

Al is impressed by Governor Strickland and Senator Brown. He thinks Brown will accomplish much in his career. He says Brown takes the time to listen to people.

Law partner Keith Belkin remembers what Al was wearing at the Sherrod Brown fundraiser.

"In 2006, we went to a fundraiser at his home for Sherrod Brown, and Al was wearing one of his Hawaiian shirts. Sherrod got up to speak and said, 'I want to thank Al for letting us use his house, and I want to thank him for wearing that shirt.' Al went through his pajama phase, through his sweatshirt phase, and through his Hawaiian shirt phase. I have no idea how he developed his sartorial taste."

Bob Luria said, "He's not a guy who blends into the woodwork. I think he probably thinks he's a good dresser."

Jordan Rothkopf said, "I sort of admire him, because he has the guts to be who he wants to be, and how he wants to be. Friends just know, that's Al. He used to be quite dapper."

Jordan got a last-minute invitation to that Sherrod Brown fundraiser at Al's house.

"Al called and said, 'I want you to come over. There's a cocktail party and there's going to be a guy here who I think is funny. I can't remember his name.' I couldn't imagine who was going to be at Al's house, so I walked into his house and there's James Carville. You never know what's going to happen when Al calls you."

Sherrod Brown also attended a reception at the Case Western Reserve Law School. The rotunda was being named in honor of Al Gray. It coincided with Al's eightieth birthday. Al has been a regular contributor to the law school.

Al said, "It's a sincere appreciation to the fact private universities have to continue to raise money, or they will be out of business. Not everyone can afford to do it. People like me, who can do it, ought to do it. The graduates owe something to the next generations."

Al met with President Ronald Reagan at the White House during meetings about Soviet Jewry.

"I think Ronald Reagan cared about freedom. He liked the concept of freedom. I think he was the smartest politician we have had in the White House, with the exception of Franklin Roosevelt. I think he was a powerful speaker and carried a lot of weight at that time. Reagan knew what to say whenever he got the microphone. I think Obama is the same way. Reagan was one of my favorite actors. I think he did some very positive things overseas. He worked with the Soviet regime. He was very good for us."

Al gives credit to Ronald Reagan for rescuing the U.S. economy.

"Jimmy Carter had taken the interest rates to 21.5% on loans. I paid that much to borrow money. How could you make money in your investments when you paid 21.5% interest to the banks or to your stock companies. I felt very disappointed in Carter and the Democratic Party."

Many see Jimmy Carter as a peace maker. He brought Egyptian President Anwar Sadat together with Israeli Prime Minister Menachem Begin in September of 1978. They agreed to the Camp David Accords. Their efforts led to the Israel-Egypt Peace treaty the following year.

"I didn't see Carter as a friend in the Middle East to American and Jewish interests. He didn't do things in a way that produced an effective result."

Al has been a supporter of open dialogue. He sponsored a long-running lecture series at the Jewish Community Center. Two-hundred-forty speakers were brought in to explore a variety of issues.

"I have supported the National Parks because I love Western travel. I support wildlife causes like the National Wildlife Federation. Supporting programs and causes makes me feel a little poorer, but I get a lot of good feeling out of helping the struggling people and animals of the world. The fish. The fish are struggling too, but I give more to human causes."

Al Gray has always celebrated the fact we live in a democracy. Americans can gather and speak out about things that trouble them.

"I'm always glad our system allows for expression. I hated what happened at Kent State. Students died at the hands of our own soldiers. Our system broke down. Our system usually does well when it comes to our conflicts."

Bob Luria thinks Al could have used his social skills to become a politician.

"He was always very interested in people. He'd talk to them about what they did, all about their family, their kids. He'd remember all of that stuff."

Al always makes note of what people are wearing. Bob Luria remembers the time a woman came into the office with some sort of outlandish scarf over her head.

"Al told her she looks so pretty in purple. She had the purple shmata over her head. The woman was by no means attractive. To tell her she looked good, I mean it made her feel good, but it certainly wasn't true."

Is Al quick to dish out compliments?

Bob Luria said, "Oh my God, to everybody. I never bother to notice what people are wearing. It's not my personality."

For most of his life, Al has been handing out compliments as if they were candy.

Al said, "In my law practice days, early on, keeping quiet was easier for me to do, but less effective for me to do as a lawyer, so I pushed myself to talk about people's appearance. I found that opening up to people, helped them open up. If you talk to somebody about their tie or their hairdo, it arouses them to a level of discussion and openness that you couldn't have had some other way. People are not used to hearing things like that. They don't know how to react, but these days, more people respond, saying they are glad I noticed what they are wearing."

Taking on the role as a compliment distributor has served Al well.

"It has helped me. Making people feel more comfortable than they did when they first shook your hand, is a good idea."

Luria says Al knows how to work a room.

"He had a way of always getting everyone involved in the conversation, whether or not they wanted to be involved. Especially now, in his later years, he could be in a room celebrating his seventy-fifth birthday, or something, and he could remember something about every single person who was attending. He could bring up something that happened forty or fifty years ago. He was pretty remarkable about doing that, I mean with every person who was there. He remembered things about all of those relationships."

Keith Belkin tips his hat to Al.

"He was always a good person to know, because he would always reach out to you and make you feel welcome."

To Market, to Market

The year was 1950. Al had just finished his second year of law school, and thought this was a good time to get into the stock market. Al's favorite local stock was Republic Steel. He bought it because every time he drove past the mill and saw those smokestacks, he felt a sense of pride. He thought he was involved emotionally with those stacks. He bought $378 worth of Republic Steel. Six dollars went to his broker from Bache, Sue Brady.

"I bought it in May, just before the beginning of the Korean War. It went to a new high. I looked like I knew what I was doing. I still have the Republic Steel annual report from that year."

He next bought shares in Southern Railway and Durez Plastics. His next purchase in 1952 certainly paid off, but Al's motivation was a little suspect.

"As a kid, I had become very interested in Holland. In second grade, I was the most important actor in a play called *A Ship to Holland*. I got to wear a captain's hat. I felt like a big shot. So in 1952, I heard of a company called Royal Dutch Petroleum. In those days, no one bought foreign stocks. It wasn't listed on the New York Stock Exchange. It was the second largest oil company in the world."

Al started buying ten shares at a time. It cost $280 plus commission each time. The stock started at twenty-eight dollars and went to forty. Al liked the feeling of earning money in the market.

"As my income improved, I did all I could to buy stock. In 1957 I bought five different aviation stocks including Douglas, Lockheed, Boeing and Northrup. I was really into airplanes. I bought just a few shares at a time. I still own Boeing and Northrup."

Al started bragging about his market prowess to other lawyers. He started giving advice to them about the market. They would call him on the phone for tips.

"I would encourage everybody to buy. It probably would have been wiser for them to save their money and only invest a proportion in stocks. It was very dangerous to put all of your money in stocks. Sometimes I prospered, sometimes I didn't. You are very vulnerable when all of your eggs are in one basket."

Al was hooked on the market. In fact, he had the confidence to borrow money to buy stocks. Buying on margin can provide even greater risk.

"I had faith in my own judgment. It's a multiplication factor. If you borrow a dollar for every dollar you have to invest, you have two dollars, and that gives you double the power when you are investing. But you better know what you are doing."

Al just figured his judgment better be right at least 51% of the time. He says that is the minimum. When you buy on margin, the broker becomes the banker. Al says the terms are favorable because the broker continues to hold the stocks as security. You don't actually hold the certificate, and they can force you to sell.

Geoff Greenleaf, of Private Harbour Investment Management says Al has never been leery of buying stocks on margin.

Geoff said, "He has used margin buying pretty well over time. Most investors don't buy on margin. Most investors, if they are making a $10,000 investment, will just put up $10,000 cash and buy a stock. Whereas if you use margin, you can put up as little as $5,000 and buy a

$10,000 dollar stock position. The nice thing about that is, if the stock goes up to $15,000, you have doubled your money. You still owe $5,000 on that, so you have gone from $5,000 initially to $10,000. The bad news is, if the stock goes down to $5,000, you have lost all of your money because you still owe the $5,000 and the stock is only worth $5,000."

Al says Douglas put commercial aviation on the map. He was enthralled with a plane called the DC-3. He says following his personal interests on Wall Street was potentially dangerous.

"I would tend to stay in one or two areas of the market. Timing has a great deal to do with stock market success. I like good quality stocks. I try to be very quality-driven. Not necessarily conservative, but I am more conservative now in my older years. I know I am not going to live forever."

Scott Fisher is Al's investment adviser at Merrill Lynch in Chagrin Falls. Scott says it's not common for investors in Al's age bracket to be so involved on a daily basis.

Scott said, "Most people are in a hands-off mode by that point. He's very hands on. He has a tremendous broad-base of knowledge, not just from the legal field where he came from, but he has strong general knowledge and good investment prowess. He has a walk-around knowledge of just about everything."

Al was never a big fan of mutual funds. He prefers to do his own management of his holdings. He listens to what his brokers have to say, but he doesn't always follow their advice.

Al's friend Alan Schonberg said, "I think he is one the true geniuses in the stock market. His ability to pick stocks, to know when to hold them, when to sell them. He is a brilliant, intuitive stock market player, and he has the guts to do it. It's a challenge for him to beat the market. Everybody loves money, and it's an ego-satisfier. He feels good being as good as he is at it."

Al's instincts can be pretty good. Toward the end of 2007, he had a feeling the market was going to plummet. Geoff Greenleaf helped him unload many of his holdings. He did a huge amount of selling to get himself out of debt.

Geoff said, "We decided which stocks to sell to reduce his margin commitment. It worked pretty well. He wound up in far better shape than he would have if he held all of those positions. The market went pretty steadily down until March of 2009. It was an eighteen-month, very severe slide of over 50% of the Dow Jones. I think his sell-off was pretty astute."

The move put Al in a position where his income tax burden soared because of the gains he realized.

Al said, "The IRS loved it, but I saved a great deal of money by liquidating, because the subsequent decline of the market would have destroyed those holdings."

Al remains a student of the stock market. He does a lot of research. He reads everything he can grab on to. He steers clear of the Internet.

"People laugh at me for not using the Internet and not being a modern thinker. I make up for it in my own way. I do things my own way. I feel it's a better way. I do rely on some of the advice I get from brokers who do use the Internet. It's just not for me."

Al was thrilled he unloaded many of his holdings before the market tanked in 2008.

"All the instincts I had, told me the market was very vulnerable. I couldn't be sure what was going to happen."

Gerry Goldberg has known Al for more than thirty years. He handles his investments at Winslow Asset Management. He has gained a lot from his relationship with Al.

"I have learned how to treat people properly. I have seen he's a man who has lifelong friendships. He has taught me the value of a very acute business sense. He has relied on a combination of curiosity, intelligence and patience. He's also got humility, or else he wouldn't ask me to help him. He's among the most colorful people I deal with, but I have a lot of colorful characters."

Geoff Greenleaf said, "I think he's got a sense of adventure to him, and that shows through in a lot of things he's done. He enjoys the thrill of the hunt and figuring out something that he perceives might do well, and then backing that relatively significantly."

Al says he gets sixty to seventy pieces of mail every day. He is buried under stacks of mail.

"Part of my house is a shambles. That's my house. It has a lot of good, and a lot of bad."

Scott Fisher said, "One of the things that sets him apart from the other clients we have, is his knack for identifying opportunities. He doesn't take a position on a company unless he really understands what the company does. That's what is supposed to happen, but rarely happens because people don't take the time, nor do they have the skill-set to really understand what they are getting into."

Al's overwhelming success on Wall Street can be attributed to the big bang theory. When he scores, he really scores.

Geoff Greenleaf said, "Al has had some big wins. Some stocks that turn out to be worth ten times what he puts in to them. When you get into something like that, you can afford to have losses in 60 or 70% of the other stocks. He goes for the big win and is willing to hold on for dear life as the stock goes up. He doesn't sell it too soon. A lot of people say they bought a stock at 25 a share, now it's 50, so I'm going to take my profits and run. That may be true, but what you can do is leave a lot of money on the table. Two years later, it could be at 250 and you kick yourself. But Al's the kind of guy who would get 250 out of it because he's willing to go through the ups and downs by taking that longer vision of it."

Al thinks the brokers differ greatly. He makes sure he stays with the ones who are good.

"I would say two out of three are good, but today it is increasingly difficult to find those two out of three. Brokers tend to be too mechanical and not judgment-oriented enough. The cost of doing business is so high for them, they just become more determined to earn commissions for themselves."

Scott Fisher said clients normally have a relationship with a broker that is based on trust. That trust builds as time goes on. Most rely heavily on their broker.

Scott said, "Al has that trust, otherwise he doesn't work with you. He is an investor who fully understands what he is getting into before he pulls the trigger. He is a student of the market."

Al said, "I like a broker who doesn't want to be in a hurry just to earn a commission, but wants to make money for his client. The brokers all have a high standard of living. The market tumbled. It has been hard for the average broker to make a living. They want to churn up your account to make commission."

Al feels comfortable paying his brokers a higher amount per transaction. By doing that, they make a little more working for him than for their average customer. They also realize he has more personal skill than most, and they find out what he is doing on his own. So they like to talk to Al. Al thinks a good broker can get as much from his clients as he does from his own research.

Scott Fisher values his relationship with Al.

"I love it. Anybody working in this field who comes up with a client who really understands what they are doing, it makes for a much more dynamic relationship than when you are trying to talk to somebody all the time, and you are kind of wondering in the back of your mind, are they really understanding what I'm saying?"

Because Al has invested so much money over the years, he is sought out by brokers. He is classified as an accredited investor because of the net worth he has accumulated. He says he gets calls from brokers who know he has money to invest.

"They tell you how good they are. They falsify in many ways. They call and say I called you six months ago and tipped you off about a stock that has since really skyrocketed. I say, oh really. I keep a list of people who called me and you are not on the list. They then say your list is bad, or say, well, at least I am on the list today."

Al's good friend Bob Silverman said, "The amazing thing about Al Gray is his ability to know more about the stock market than anybody on Wall Street. Al was in the psychiatric hospital for some months, and during that entire time, the one thing he had no problem with is the stock market. He still had control of that."

Bob said he did "fabulous" with one stock Al recommended to him. Several times he asked Al if he would manage his money for him.

Geoff Greenleaf says Al's hard work pays off.

"He's not a closet indexer. That is someone who owns a lot of stocks, but when you boil it all down, they are almost in proportion to the Standard & Poor's 500 stock index. They are not going to do much worse or much better than the S&P 500. Whereas Al will take significant positions in individual securities without regard to how they are going to do compared to the market. My sense is he has done better than the market over the last fifty years because of that."

Al says it is not unusual to get five cold calls from brokers every day.

"If I get a lot of calls from brokers in a short period of time, I think the market is about to reach a temporary top. It's going to stop going up and start going down because you are getting so many calls telling you how great it is. To me that is a negative indication."

Al believes it is very easy to be a buyer. It is much more difficult to be a seller. The stories of reasons to buy are much more prevalent, but it is much harder to decide when it is time to sell.

Al says he devotes fifty to sixty hours a week to working the stock market.

"Some would say I am greedy. Others would say I want the estate I leave to be in as good of shape as possible, and that my heirs and charities will benefit from all of my work. Besides I love it!"

Geoff Greenleaf said, "I recently signed up a client who was seventy-eight and said he didn't want to do it anymore. He said he'd rather spend time doing other things. Al still loves it. It keeps his mind active."

Most investors in Al's age bracket ease away from stock holdings and put their money into bonds because they are less of a risk.

Geoff Greenleaf said, "What you should do is take your age and subtract it from 100, and that will determine what percentage you should have in common stocks. An eighty-two year old should have

18% in common stock. Al's got a very heavy portion of his liquid net worth in common stock, which does set him apart. He's the exact opposite of that rule of thumb."

Al's success in the stock market and his love of playing the game, were the significant reasons he pulled away from practicing law. Scott Fisher says investing has become Al's second career. It's like having a full-time job.

Scott said, "Every morning, we go over his holdings. We go over developments in the news. We look at opportunities we see coming forward. Invariably, it will lead to a discussion about a life situation he has experienced."

Scott is impressed by Al's incredible courage in his investment activity.

Scott said, "I think it's something you've got to be born with. I don't think anyone can teach you. I think he is comfortable with himself. He doesn't stick his neck out so far on any one thing that it's going to hurt him. He figures out what he can afford to lose if a stock goes bad. He's not afraid to take a risk, but he's also not afraid to laugh at himself when things don't go well."

Scott Fisher said Al has become a big part of his life.

"There is always something you can, and should learn from what he's telling you. I learn from him every day. It's not necessarily things relating to the stock market. It's things about life in general. The man is on the ball. He knows what's going on out in the world. He is a pleasure to talk with."

Geoff Greenleaf sings Al's praises, as well.

"He's eclectic. He's interested in all kinds of things. He's quite an engaging conversationalist. He's very much alive. He's a very engaging person. He's not a wallflower. He doesn't go into a cocoon as many people do when they hit their eighties. He's the kind of guy who makes you feel good to be around."

Taking Stock of a Broker

On a summer day, Al made the trip from his home in Moreland Hills, to his stockbroker's office on Landerbrook Drive in Mayfield Heights. Fintegra Financial Solutions occupies a prominent place, just off the front lobby of the attractive mid-rise building. Al had to come in to handle some paperwork.

Jim Unger is one of his brokers.

"Al and technology are not necessarily friendly. He would get faxes and have them sent here. I would put them in the mail, or drop them off at his house. I bought him a fax machine. I think it is still in the box in his office."

On this day, it was difficult for Al to slip into Fintegra unnoticed. He was attired in a red and blue cabana suit. It was suitable for a day at the pool at the Fontainebleau Hotel in Miami, but was by no means business wear.

Jim said, "I have always equated Al Gray to a guy who buys a Porshe 911 in some hideous color. He is so comfortable in his own skin. He could give a damn about what the rest of the world thinks. He's a character. There's not another Al Gray."

Jim and his wife Kelly were among those on hand when Al was honored at the Case Western Reserve Law School. The atrium of the building was being named for him.

"He comes to the event in a shirt you could probably vomit upon and not notice. He wore a blue velour jacket, something Hugh Hefner would wear. No one looked askance at him. It was an un-Godly paisley shirt. This guy has his own sense of style."

Jim Unger and Al Gray have a special relationship. Jim talks to Al, two or three times a day. Handling Al's accounts, requires 12 to 15% of Jim's daily workload. Al has mentored Jim in his career. They have become friends, confidants. Jim jokingly says they are married. Their lives are intertwined. Al came into Jim's life at an important time.

"My father, Stanford Unger, died about the time I met Al, so he filled a fatherly role for me whenever I had business issues or moral issues."

It was about that time, Jim got a call from his birth mother. Jim was twenty-eight. He had always known he was adopted. His birth mother was dying. She had never bothered to call him before. Jim was able to talk to her on the phone for ninety minutes before she passed.

Jim and Kelly were about to be married. There were a lot of changes in his life in a short time. Al assumed a special role.

Jim said. "I've got a soft spot for the guy, and I'll do whatever he needs done. It feels real good to be there for him. When Al tells me I did a good job, it's better than the 200 bucks I earned on the trade. That puts me in a good mood for a week."

Al's involvement with the stock market is like a full-time job. Jim says there are occasional weeks when Al will devote just five minutes to his accounts, but many weeks he may invest eighty hours of his time poring over stock charts.

Jim provides Al with insights about the market, but Al brings a lot of his own knowledge to the table. How often does Jim follow Al's lead and add stocks to his own portfolio that Al has recommended?

"Virtually always, if he can convince me enough. He will expect me to poke every hole in an idea. He doesn't expect me to agree with him. He wants me to be the devil's advocate. I have been working with him for twelve years, and my pulse rate still gets up when we are getting into it hot and heavy, whether a certain stock should be bought. If I am wrong, he will pick up on it. He wants me to be an old-school broker."

Jim says when Al wins the battle, and convinces Jim about a certain stock, he will share Al's views with some of his other clients. They are familiar with Al's track record, and often hop aboard.

Jim admits his dealing with Al has made him a better broker and a wealthier man.

"He has enabled me to see more clearly, to not just react to a first impression. He is not my most lucrative client, but he has certainly improved my financial position greatly by making me better at my job. He has given me great advice, some of which has been hard to receive. It has always improved my business acumen. Of all the clients I have had, no one has taught me more about the business than Al, in terms of charting out a stock position, to understanding the psychology of a client."

Al has CNBC blaring in his home most of the day, but without Internet access, he researches stock trends the old-fashioned way. He buries himself in a stack of mail everyday. He reads finance-related publications religiously.

Jim said, "I think it has probably helped him. We have become so used to up-to-the-minute data in making decisions in a micro-second. Somebody who takes the time to take a step back, perhaps gets a chance to think about information and oftentimes, makes better decisions than the guys flying by the seat of their pants. I don't have another client whose portfolios do as well as his do."

Jim say Al is able to apply his life lessons to his decision-making process. He says his keen knowledge of history also works to his advantage.

"The day George W. Bush was declared the winner for his first term, Al called and placed hundred-thousand dollar orders on five defense stocks. Al told me, 'We are getting a redneck from Texas, and I am guessing you are going to see major expenditures on defense.' Not a one of those stocks has less than quadrupled in the last nine years."

Jim says Al has the ability to cut through the fluff and get to the heart of real issues. He credits his understanding of people. Jim thinks Al's experience as a lawyer has helped him think rationally.

"There are a hundred defense companies. Why did he choose the five he chose?"

Jim says Al is often able to spot a stock's potential before others can. He zeroed in on a biochemical firm called Enzo. It was a startup company, and Al liked what he saw.

Jim said, "He found out about the company. He did a lot of research and took down a large position in the stock. He was probably a year and a half early on that stock and to this day, that has probably been his biggest winner. That victory enabled him to invest more in the Al Gray style. He had enough money to cast his net wide enough, and in the direction he wanted to improve his performance."

Al is no shrinking violet. He has the guts to put large sums of money on the line. When others take a woe-is-me attitude about their losses in the market, Al blazes ahead and invests even more money.

"There's blood in the streets, and he's buying. A year ago, when things were at their worst, I'd have ten sell-tickets and one buy-ticket, and the buy was Al. He bought Goldman Sachs in the spring of 2009. The stock was under 100, and now it's over 200. He had no fear. He respects the leadership of a company. He is not afraid to take losses. He'll say he was wrong on this one, let's go. He's also able to say maybe I wasn't wrong on this stock, but perhaps a little early. I'll wait it out."

When Al determines it's time to pull the trigger, he blazes ahead.

Jim said. "I've watched him as a big boy, take some big losses. No issue, no thought. No mention of it. What's next?"

When the stock market has taken a major nosedive, Jim sometimes feels like crawling under his desk. Al has encouraged him to keep in touch with his clients even when the news is bad. He says those clients would rather get the details from their broker than read about them in the paper the next day.

Jim thinks Al has all the compassion in the world, yet has little tolerance for fools. He is eager to help someone with guidance in a business project, but is not impressed by people who have no motivation and just expect a handout.

Jim has come to know what keeps Al as a player in the stock market.

"Making money is a nice thing, but I think his motivation is finding something before anybody else does. It's spotting a trend, or seeing an idea before others. It gives him a thrill. The day Al slows down, a little, he'll slow down completely. He's too curious about too much."

Jim Unger owes a lot to Al Gray. Their friendship has changed the course of Jim's life. He has unwavering respect for Al.

"This is a man who came from nothing. He's given back immensely. This is a man who could have been selfish."

Jim Unger thinks when Al's father disappeared, Al had to look elsewhere for approval.

"The most important thing to Al isn't the trappings of success, but the perception of him in the community. He enjoys the feeling of being well-received in the community."

.

Enola Gay

The *Enola Gay* was the B-29 Superfortress aircraft that was used to drop the atomic bomb on Hiroshima in August 1945, at the end of World War II.

Al said, "After the war ended, the *Enola Gay* was put in storage in the desert in Arizona. It was totally rusted. To be restored, it had to be sent in two pieces to a facility in Maryland."

The restoration work got underway in 1984. Al got involved in the project in 1997 when he provided funds to complete the work. He is listed as the official restorer of the aircraft. In December 2003, The plane was placed in the new Smithsonian Air and Space Museum's Steven F. Udvar-Hazy Center in Chantilly, Virginia near Dulles Airport. Al was honored at a black-tie dinner held at Dulles to commemorate the restoration.

Al said, "I was overwhelmed by the opportunity to shake hands with the pilot of the plane, Col. Paul Tibbets. It was a celebrity evening. There were many prominent people there. It was a big-time event."

The restoration of the *Enola Gay* touched off a good deal of controversy. Was the plane a symbol of man's inhumanity to man, or did it represent America's determination to put an end to the war and prevent millions of military and civilian deaths?

Al said, "There are people who say it was a mistake to drop the atomic bomb. Had the bomb not been dropped, that war would have gone on another year. Perhaps two or three million lives would have been lost on both sides. Restoring the plane was the most appropriate thing the museum could have done. I was proud to be involved. There are always going to be naysayers, but when you are talking about saving millions of lives, I don't know how you can criticize it. The Japanese were not about to surrender. Hirohito was not about to surrender. Tojo was not going to give in. He would have had the war go on as long as possible, regardless of the loss of life. Can you imagine how many people would have died had there been a full invasion of Japan?"

The Boeing B-29 Superfortress was the most sophisticated propeller-driven bomber of its time. It was the first bomber to have pressurized compartments for the eleven-man flight crew. The *Enola Gay's* restoration was the most extensive in Smithsonian history. It was in poor condition. Corrosion was painstakingly removed. More than 300,000 staff hours were needed to bring the aircraft back to its original glory.

When it first went on display, the director of the Smithsonian Air and Space Museum, Gen. J.R. "Jack" Dailey said, "Future generations will sense first-hand the unalterable significance of the aircraft in World War II and human history."

Al also supplied funds for the restoration of one of his favorite World War II fighters, the single-seat, Hawker Hurricane. It was a key component of the Battle of Britain. The Hawker Hurricanes were used to shoot down the invading German bombers. More than three thousand Nazi warplanes were turned back by 688 British planes. The Hawker Hurricane was debuted in 1935. It was small and fast. Early models had cloth-covered fuselages. Al is so proud of his Hawker tie-in that the vanity license plate on his car spells out HAWKER.

Arlene Fine, a reporter for the *Cleveland Jewish News* was in Virginia for the dedication of the Smithsonian's Udvar-Hazy Center. She said Al was in his glory.

"The grand-opening gala was phenomenal. They introduced Al and some other major donors. It was the most incredible experience. You had Washington VIPs, and retired Air Force pilots who had made history. The pilots of the Enola Gay were there. It was really a historic event. It was a huge thing for Al Gray. There he was next to the *Enola Gay*. When you consider that was the plane that dropped the bomb on Hiroshima, it was pretty impressive."

Al's friend Wynell accompanied him to the dedication. The two were elegantly dressed. It was a special evening.

Arlene said, "Al was just as happy as could be. He was very, very proud. He was given the royal VIP treatment. He likes history. He's a history buff. He felt he was part of a historic moment in American history. In some small way, he was connected to it. When you are a collector and a history buff, this is a very significant event in your memory book."

Al said, "It was history. It was a tremendous thing. I was shaking hands with history. I'm very proud to have my name on the monument to Hiroshima."

J.R. "Jack" Dailey said about Al, "Thank you for your support of National Air and Space Museum projects, including *The Wright Brothers & the Invention of the Aerial Age* and the restoration of artifacts in the collection. We are grateful for your continued commitment to the Museum over the years and are fortunate to count you as a friend."

Al's friend Jordan Rothkopf knew about Al's involvement with restoring the *Enola Gay*. He went to visit the Udvar-Hazy Center.

"I had heard about Al's involvement years before, and I kind of put it in the back of my mind. So, when I went to museum, and saw the *Enola Gay* with his name on the plaque, I was overwhelmed."

Someday, Al's grandson Azzizi will be taken to the museum to take a look at his grandfather's name next to the *Enola Gay*.

Geoff Hanks said, "When Azzizi was born, we realized there was no one to carry on the Gray name. Rachel and I decided to honor Al by giving Azzizi the last name Gray. When he looks at his grandfather's name next to the *Enola Gay*, he will be able to make a direct connection to him. We wanted to honor Al by carrying on his last name."

Vietnam

"I'm a pro-American patriot of the greatest order. Vietnam was a civil war in my mind. It was a tough choice for Washington to get involved, but it was an understandable choice. South Vietnam was not as democratic as I thought it should be. I didn't like the loss of life. It was a very heavy loss of life."

The extended Gray family was hit hard by the war, not on the battlefields, but here in Cleveland.

Al's older brother Lou and his wife Ruth raised their family on Bayard Road in South Euclid. They had four children, Joel, Eliott, Kim and Carol.

Eliott and Joel both served in Vietnam. What they had seen there had changed their outlook on life. Depression was setting in. It was before many people were noticing the terrible psychological impact the war was having on our soldiers.

Al said, "Eliott was in a car playing Russian roulette with another fellow. Eliott was killed. His friend ran from the car. It happened in South Euclid.

"Joel's suicide was in 1968. He killed himself in his grandmother's garage. Vietnam left him with mental wounds from what he had seen over there and what he had done over there. He was a Green Beret."

Al says, not surprisingly, his nephew Kim was affected by the tragic deaths of his brothers. It left him with scars psychologically.

"These fine young men were favorites of mine. We were very close. My brother and sister-in-law were overwhelmed. I tried to get them to get counseling. In fact, I made several appointments, but they were not interested in seeking any remedies. It was less common back then for people to seek help. I think my brother Louis took it the hardest. Ruth was able to find a way to cope with the losses."

Al remembers the anti-war protests that divided our nation.

"I've been proud of freedoms and the right to protest. I was not about to march in the war protests, but I was supportive of the right to do so. I believe in our legal system. I still recognize the shortcomings in our world politics. Vietnam was a tough one."

Al and Anita traveled to London during the Vietnam war. They were attending a formal dinner in Guild Hall. Each table at the banquet had a British host.

Anita said, "It was a very proper kind of dinner. This British host started assailing the United States, and that's nothing you want to happen in front of Al Gray. Al just took off on this guy. There were other Americans there sitting on their hands. Al did it in an elegant, sophisticated way. The guy was just brutalized, mortified and was proven to be the jerk he was."

Al, small in stature, was never one to back down from a confrontation. Lottie remembers they were driving on Warrensville Center Road. Some teenagers were in a car ahead of them and the driver was being reckless.

"My dad got out of his car and confronted the teenagers. Who would get out and confront anyone? My dad is very confident and assertive. When others might not take that step. He takes that step."

Then there was that time Al and his family were walking to a Browns game. Some young tough guys were swearing up a storm.

Rachel said, "My dad walked up to them and said you've just got to stop, and clean up your language. These kids just said okay."

On the Road Again

"I love the United States. It's an absolutely fabulous place to spend your life. I'm proud to be a Cleveland resident. Proud to be a supporter of Cleveland, and to enjoy everything about Cleveland. I think I have made a difference to the total community and especially to the Jewish community."

Al certainly enjoys living in Cleveland, but he has never passed on a chance to travel to all corners of the Earth.

He was a nineteen-year-old kid when he took his first airplane ride. He hopped aboard a DC-3 at Midway Airport in Chicago and flew to Detroit. He thinks the fare was seven dollars. The Cleveland Indians were playing a doubleheader, and Al arranged to meet one of his friends there.

"It was one of the most exciting things ever. I loved the airplane, and here I was flying on an airplane. By today's standards, it was pretty primitive. The seats were plain. The DC-3 first went into service in 1937. It became the workhorse of the airlines for many years."

In 1959, Al set out on a more substantial journey. He went to South America for thirty days. He went to Peru and to the ancient city of Machu Picchu. He learned too late, on that trip not to drink the water and he became quite ill with a bad case of tourista.

"It was as repulsive an illness as I ever had."

The following year, he made his trip to Europe aboard an Italian ocean liner.

In 1962, Al took his first around the world trip. Turkey, Greece, Israel, Pakistan, India, Nepal, Thailand, Hong Kong, and Taiwan. It culminated with a week-long stay in Japan, visiting Osaka, Tokyo, and Kyoto.

"All of the war damage was gone. Tokyo was crowded as heck, but probably half the size it is now. I was impressed things were back to normal. It was an exciting city. The occupation after the war ended, and they weren't accustomed to seeing many Americans then. I was proud of what they had accomplished. The war was gone. They were thinking about another world."

Al has been back two times since, and would like to go again.

Al developed strong financial ties to Japan. He started buying stock there in the '60s.

"Tokyo Marine is an insurance company. You could not beat what its stock did. It seemed like it was going up every day."

Al loaded up on Matsushita before it took off. His Japanese holdings tapered off in the late '80s.

"There was a world economic crisis in 1987. I saw my Japanese stocks tanking. I didn't want to ride them down. Japan has never been as financially effective as it was before 1987. I still have a few shares of my Japanese stocks that I used to own in big numbers. I didn't want to divest myself emotionally from them."

Al says the Japanese government misunderstood what was going on with the economy in the '80s. Things got botched up and never fully got back on track.

Al and Anita took their children to Israel many times. Al has taken Lottie to Europe. He has invited Rachel along on trips to Ecuador and the Galapagos Islands.

Rachel said, "Even in kindergarten I remember thinking how lucky I was. Most kids didn't get to go to those places."

Anita says it would have been easier to leave the kids back home when they traveled, but didn't want the children to miss out.

"They see the world. It's easier to understand their place in the world. We thought it was a fabulous educational experience for them. We wanted them to understand their place in the world. You are not just a citizen of the United States. You are a citizen of the world."

Al's niece, Carol Marger's earliest memories of her uncle is his thirst for world travel.

"When I was growing up, he was always traveling. He would always come back with gifts for us from South America, Asia, and Europe. It was very exotic. He had an exotic lifestyle."

Al said, "All my life, I wanted to go to Antarctica. I went in November of 2004. The weather at that time there was the equivalent of our spring, but it was severe."

To get to Antarctica, he traveled from Argentina aboard a Russian icebreaker. The seas were rocky the whole time.

"Back and forth as much as you would ever want a ship to rock. In fact, a little more than you would want it to rock."

Al and his fellow travelers spent four or five days visiting penguin colonies and scientific research stations.

"It was considered mild for that part of the world. Twenties in the daytime, and it got down below zero at night. It was a super trip. One of the best ever. The boat trip was grueling. You didn't think the boat trip would ever end."

Al and his shipmates fared better than Polar explorer Ernest Shackleton. He got stuck in the frozen waters of Antarctica's Weddell Sea in January of 1915. The following October, with ice floes pressing against his ship, Shackleton ordered his crew to abandon it. They were camped out on an ice floe. One month later, the ship sank. The men were eventually rescued, but had gone 497 days without stepping on solid ground.

Al's dining room features a picture of Shackleton's ship Endurance. There is also a photo of the explorer, along with his autograph. The photo of the ship was taken while it was frozen in the ice.

Shackleton's adventures in the cold were definitely a hot topic on the trip. Shackleton's great nephew from Holland was among those traveling with Al.

"The trip makes you view your own life a bit differently. It made me appreciate my life in Cleveland. I like my lifestyle. I think I have been very fortunate to live in one community, know it as well as I do, and love it as much as I do."

Carol Marger has fond memories of being included in Al's travels. When she was living with a family in Switzerland, she met Al in Geneva. When Al and his family were traveling to London aboard the Queen Elizabeth 2, he invited Carol along to help care for Lottie and Rachel. Carol loved the cruise and the visit to London. He has taken Carol to Israel two times. Al made a point to meet up with Carol and take in all the sights when she lived in New York, California, and Florida.

She said, "He encouraged me to do my own travels. He did exciting things. My uncle likes to grab the opportunity. He will create a situation. He'll stay at wonderful hotels. He likes to find the best restaurants. If you are with him, you are going to do these things, too. His love of travel became something he could share with me."

The Other Al Gray

With airline security being what it is today, you wonder if the ticket agent at Hopkins Airport was taken aback when a couple of guys walked up to the counter both named Al Gray. This couldn't be a father and son combination. One Al Gray was eighty-one, the other was seventy-six.

The younger Al Gray was heading down to Dallas in August of 2009 to celebrate the eightieth birthday of his sister Rita. She was a long-time school principal in Texas. Rita made sure her favorite cousin Alvie was invited to come along.

Two-hundred-fifty guests would gather for the birthday tribute to Rita Gray. A brunch was held the following morning. Her brother Alan and her cousin Alvie both stood up and shared memories of the Gray family. Rita said Alvie "held the guests spellbound." It was a glorious weekend. Sadly, it would be the last time Rita would see her beloved brother.

Just a couple of months later, Alan was with a group of friends. They would always gather on Sunday mornings to walk dogs from an animal shelter. He was out with a dog when Alan's heart gave out and he died.

Al said, "The death of my cousin Alan Gray brings to mind the whole subject of our lives. When you get to my age, you are a lot more conscious. It is so frequent now that the people you spent your life with are suddenly taken from your life."

Alan Gray's father was Morris Gray. He was a dentist with an office at E. 93rd and Hough. Alan grew up on Rossmoor in Cleveland Heights. He was a good athlete. A champion swimmer. Later on, he would become a downhill skier. He was an outdoorsman. He loved to go fishing.

"He used to call himself the 'other' Al Gray."

Al wasn't home the Sunday morning of Alan's death. When he came home he found a message on his answering machine from his nephew in California. He was inquiring if it would be okay if his mother Rita could stay at Al's house when she came in town for the funeral. At that point, he didn't even know there had been a death in the family.

Al called Alan's wife Carol. He assumed that Alan had died.

"She said this has been the worst morning ever."

Alan and Carol had been married fifty-five years.

Al said, "Losing someone now is not an unusual experience. It gets to be an everyday occurrence. Of course, your own life has to be considered at risk too."

The funeral would be held two days later at Berkowitz-Kumin in Cleveland Heights. Rabbi Joshua Skoff challenged mourners to measure up to Alan Gray.

"Did you pursue all of the potential of your life? Did you fill your life with meaning? His hands were busy and his mind was busy. He was serious about everything. He was the eternal optimist. He was like an eternal student. He was always eager to share. He would get the most out of life each day."

His son-in-law, Ben Hornstein, said Alan taught him important lessons. Take on your own responsibilities.

"Pack your own chute. You can't wait for good things to happen to you. You must seek those out. He never sat idly by, waiting for life to come to him. Live in the moment. When an opportunity presents itself, go for it. You rarely get a second chance to do special things with those you love. Do for others."

Alan's son, Dr. Neil Gray, said, "He had a love of animals. He loved adventure. He said complaining was a waste of time. He said childhood never ends. You can never have enough friends. Life is a gift, not to be wasted."

Rabbi Skoff praised Alan.

"He was busy with his heart. He was the most compassionate human being. That's what fueled his energy. His heart was his guide and his compass. He wanted responsibility, and he took it on. If there was a mitzvah to be found, he found it. He loved seeing others develop their skills. He took pleasure in seeing other's gains. He knew we are all responsible for one and other. He made those around him better."

Alan Gray's favorite movie was *Harold and Maude.* He said the film taught us not to dwell on past hurts and failures. Reach out. Take a chance. Play as long as you can.

Al Gray said, "A great guy has been taken from us. He was loving, kind, and generous. A nice guy."

Alan Gray's sister Rita Gray Newman was able to touch many lives as well. She was principal of a couple of award-winning elementary schools in tough neighborhoods in Dallas. She was committed to her students.

She said, "If we are going to have a city worth having, then you have to educate all children."

Not surprisingly, many of the people Rita Gray Newman inspired, came to celebrate her eightieth birthday. She was thrilled to be with her beloved brother Alan for what would turn out to be their last moments together, and grateful her cousin Alvie joined them as well.

"Alvie was a very important part of everything we did that weekend. We had a wonderful time being with him. He gave speeches and was interested in everyone and everything."

Rita says she has a wall in her home in Dallas that features numerous family pictures. They depict her parents, aunts and uncles, and her three sons.

"The picture of cousin Alvie is the only cousin on the wall," she said.

Alvie has a special place on that wall and a special place in her life.

"He's a family person. He reaches out in so many directions with such a good heart."

Rita moved to Dallas from Cleveland in 1963.

"I have never gone to Cleveland without making sure I see Alvie."

Hair Today, Gone Sixty Years Ago

Al walks into the May-Som building in Mayfield Heights. It's an unimpressive structure, probably built in the early '50s. The first left turn leads him into a place called Complete Image of Hair Design. Matt Gambatese has spent much of his life working here. He called the business MJG and Company when he owned it. A few years ago, he sold it to a couple of employees, but still works there.

Al Gray is one of Matt's most loyal and long-lasting customers. Al was fitted for his first hairpiece way back in 1948. The wig shop was located in downtown Cleveland back then, run by John E. Jevnikar.

Jevnikar came to this country in 1917 and learned to be a wigmaker. He stitched his way to becoming a master wigmaker. In 1937, he opened his own shop. John hired Matt Gambatese in 1966, and four years later, Jevnikar sold the business to his protégé. Matt moved the business from downtown to its current suburban location in 1987.

So, Al Gray has a history with the company that now exceeds sixty-one years.

Shelves in a storage room in the back section of the shop are filled with what are called blocks. These blocks are made out of wood. They are the size of a human head. Each is custom-made to reflect the exact size and shape of the head of the customer. The first step in having a hairpiece made is forming the wooden block. A paper covering is then applied to the wooden block before it is used to design the hairpiece.

Matt reaches up to a shelf that's a little higher than eye-level. He grabs one of the blocks. A metal tag with the number seventy-six is attached to the head. The number looks like something you would be given when you check your coat at a restaurant. The Al Gray head is, in a sense, the cornerstone of this business. It dates back six decades, through three different ownerships. When Al wants to have a new wig made, the wooden block will be used to make sure the new hairpiece is sized perfectly.

Al recognizes the value of his wooden head.

"Take good care of that," he says.

Many of the blocks in the shop are hand-fashioned antiques. In the early days of the business, John Jevnikar couldn't afford to buy new blocks. So he would track down old wooden crates. He sawed the crates into small pieces of wood. He would then skillfully form the head-like blocks by gluing pieces of wood together. The blocks here are relics of days gone by. By recycling the crates, Jevnikar was ahead of his time.

Al is due for a redo. He replaces his wig every year. He shells out about a thousand dollars for each one.

"Matt said, "When you see the detailed work, you would think we should charge more for a hairpiece."

When Al tells Matt he is ready for a new piece, either Carmella or Amelia will stitch his new rug. They sit next to each other in the backroom of the shop. Their work is painstakingly precise. They peer through illuminated magnifying glasses that are about the size of a dessert plate. The magnifying glasses are mounted on metal arms that can be shifted into place.

Matt says, "These women have been with me for twenty years. They are the third set of women in the company's history. They used to be seamstresses before they became wigmakers."

Al comes in once a week. Matt trims the rim of real hair Al still has. That hair is gray, and very fine. Matt shapes up Al's wig for him, and then shaves Al's face with a straight-razor. Matt says Al is the only customer he still shaves.

Matt jokingly says, "While he's in the room, I can say he's a great guy. He's a very generous man. When he walks in, everybody says, 'Hello, Mr. Gray.' I've been out to dinner with him, and no matter where we go, it's the same thing."

Al has never intended to cover up the fact he wears a rug.

"I talk about it. I don't say, how do you like my haircut? I say how do you like my hairpiece? I have two. One is a back-up, in case the other one blows away."

Al has plenty of experience buying hairpieces. He bought his first one while he was still in college.

"I bought it the day after Truman beat Dewey in the 1948 election. I was driving my dad's car to a wig guy and they were reporting the election returns on the radio."

Al started losing his hair at age fifteen.

"I thought I inherited the family trait, but got it a bit early. My dad and all of his brothers were bald. I knew there was a probability I would be bald by thirty. I didn't think I would be bald by twenty."

Al was asked if wearing a rug has hampered his ability to attract women.

"I thought it was always best to announce that I had a hairpiece, whether it looked good or not. That was helpful. It showed a willingness to admit to a weakness. A lot of guys don't like to admit they have anything wrong in their whole life."

What keeps Al's hairpiece in place, even on the windiest of days?

Matt said, "It's double-sided tape, made especially for hairpieces. Because it comes in contact with the skin, it has to be medically approved. You can't just use Scotch tape or carpet tape. Carpet tape is caustic to the skin."

Matt says the wigs he sells are 100% hand-made. It's all human hair. If someone wants a wig with touches of gray, or perhaps blonde highlights, the wigmakers assemble the various colors stand by strand.

They don't start out with just one hair color and attempt to dye portions of the wig.

A good number of the customers are women.

Matt said, "It's surprising how many women wear hairpieces. There is something called female-pattern baldness. They lose their hair all over the scalp. You get to see their whole scalp through their thinning hair. It's more important for women to get a hairpiece. Men can walk around without hair, but for women, it's not socially acceptable."

More men than ever are shaving their heads in order to make a fashion statement. Matt says trends come and go. He says the original owner of the company told him he did a strong business at the height of the Great Depression.

"During the Depression, when you thought it would be depressed for everybody, the hairpiece business was solid. People needed to look better to keep their jobs. They needed to maintain their youthful look. The first thing that would turn people off is if you looked too old for a job."

Matt and his staff have changed Al's hairpiece design numerous times. Hairstyles change and the materials used for the base of the hairpiece are upgraded.

Al and Matt's friendship goes back to 1966. Four years ago, Matt moved back to Little Italy, his childhood neighborhood. He lives in a house on E. 124th Street. It was his grandmother's house. Matt's father was born raised there. Matt is active in the community, serving on the board of the neighborhood's original settlement facility, Alta House.

He and Al share stories about the early days of Little Italy.

Matt said, "You could walk out of your house, go to the corner, and get anything you wanted. There was a hardware store, bakeries, clothing stores. And a unique thing there, three of the stores were Jewish-owned. The clothing store I worked in there was owned by Louie Shore. He could speak better Italian than my mother. His son Hymie eventually took over the business. It was located in the building where Mama Santa's restaurant is now. There was Palevsky's Hardware. It was a little store. You'd walk in and the wooden floor would creak. The building that houses Corbo's Bakery was a Jewish-owned furniture store."

As Matt finishes shaving Al's face, they reminisce about a mutual friend, Sam Guarino.

Al said, "Sam's father died. His mother was partially disabled. When Sam graduated from Case, he went into the family restaurant business instead of becoming an engineer. He was a very bright guy. He was an intelligent guy. He died too young."

Guarino's Restaurant remains a Murray Hill fixture. It first opened its doors in 1918.

Matt Gambatese's business card isn't the standard size. It is a fold-over style. The base of the card is slightly larger. It shows a man with a bald pate. Fold the smaller top portion over the base, and the man depicted suddenly has a full head of hair.

The name of this wig business has changed several times over the decades, but one thing has remained constant, Al Gray.

So, with more than sixty years experience of putting a lid on, has Al gotten pretty adept at it?

"I can do it in the dark."

Staying Fit

April is one of Al's two personal fitness trainers. He is lucky he doesn't have to spell April's last name very often. But when he writes a check to her, he no doubt has to pause as he scrawls her last name. Margagliotti.

April is thirty-one and is in top shape herself.

She said, "Back years ago, physical fitness wasn't as relevant in people's lives as it is now. We start younger, and it becomes part of our life. You are never too old to start."

Al has never been afraid to re-invent himself. Seven years ago, he enlisted the services of a personal trainer named Melanie Polk. Al didn't have to search high and low for his first trainer. Melanie is the daughter of his accountant David Polk.

Melanie said, "I was twenty-three when I signed up for a weightlifting class at the Jewish Community Center. I found out I loved it. I decided to get certified as a weight-lifting instructor. Then I hired a personal trainer and decided I wanted to be trainer. I have done it for eleven years now."

Melanie trains Al two days a week at his house. April trains him two more days a week.

April said, "It only improves the quality of life. We work on energy levels, balance and strength. When you are older, you are more at risk of falling and breaking something. Your bones are weaker. Your muscles are weaker."

Al said, "You can't lecture people, but I am prepared to share a message with everyone about the importance of good health, and the recognition at any age, you are capable of doing these things, and doing them well. I'd like to be around twelve years from now, and see my grandson's Bar Mitzvah."

Melanie and April spend an hour per session with Al. Before he started exercising, Al's weight had soared to 192 pounds. He was thrilled he got his weight down to 170, but then was diagnosed with diabetes. That made his commitment to good health even stronger.

Lottie said, "He was on meds, he gained weight, and wasn't as active as he used to be. Once he got diagnosed with diabetes, he really got into a regimen of eating right and his exercise increased. I think it's fabulous. Many people don't see a problem with diabetes, but it's a slow, silent killer. To be at his age, and in such great physical shape, is amazing."

Al said, "My goal was getting rid of as much fat as I could. I limit vodka and wine because of the sugar content. I cheat, but I don't cheat excessively. Back in the day when I was a busy young lawyer, it was difficult to wake up early in the morning and do exercise. I wanted to get downtown to work. I worked very hard and put in long hours. I was never afraid of work."

April said, "He definitely gives one hundred percent and he enjoys it. That's the most important part of it."

Al's work with his trainers has paid off nicely. He is now under 150 pounds.

Melanie said, "I would absolutely, without a doubt, without any hesitation, say he is at the top of the list in terms of his motivation, his drive, his desire to want to do it, and his commitment to doing it. He doesn't waver."

Arlene Fine said, "I knew him when he was very heavy. He was fifty pounds heavier. That's no small potatoes for someone his age to do an hour of exercise with a trainer four days a week."

Al said, "Sugar is the worst for your weight, and when you are a diabetic, it's bad for your sugar count. I brag about my weight loss all the time. I try to be subtle with people about their weight, but it's not an easy thing to be subtle about it. You have to be able to figure out ways to give messages to those you love."

He has to check his blood five times a week because of his diabetes.

April said, "His weight is controlled. His diabetes is controlled. He's pain-free for the most part. He may have a flare-up now and then, but his recovery is much quicker."

He likes to stay mentally sharp, as well.

"I read the *Plain Dealer, Wall Street Journal* and the *New York Times* every day. I read financial publications like *Barron's*. I try to broaden my knowledge. I spend three or four hours a day reading."

Melanie is amazed how Al stays so sharp mentally.

"He has an uncanny ability to remember numbers and dates and things. He can tell you about his first day of kindergarten, as well as who the teacher was and what grades he got in school."

When Al was heavy, he was pretty reckless.

"I was in my early days. I was drinking more than I should. Before and after dinner were my risk periods. Having a couple of drinks makes you hungrier. I think the secret to weight control is to make your mid-day meal your heaviest meal. Make your dinner a bit lighter."

Anita said, "Al has a sturdy constitution. I think the fact that he is taking better care of himself now more than ever, is phenomenal. He's got young children and he's now got a grandchild. He wants to stay around as long as he can."

Al thinks his physical workouts have paid off with his mental abilities. He is convinced there is a significant relationship between the mental and physical.

April said, "He's always ready to go. He has warmed up on the elliptical before I arrive. It warms up his body and loosens up his muscles. It increases his heart rate."

April has been committed to physical fitness for years.

"I started working out with friends. I liked it. I got results, and took it to the next level. I turned my hobby into my career. I have always been into a healthy lifestyle. This is a part-time job with full-time pay."

Melanie said, "I was a competitive bodybuilder. I won bodybuilding competitions in 1998 and 1999. In 2000, I won the state of Ohio bench press championship. I pressed 185 pounds."

Not surprisingly, Melanie is a big proponent of weight-training.

"Any weight-bearing exercise that you do helps increase bone density, and the loss of bone density is what affects so many older people in terms of their posture and their inability to pursue activities that they are used to doing. It's vital."

Melanie is powerful. If Al got out of line, could she take him down?

"I know I could. So far he's been a good boy."

April supervises the workouts for her clients like Al, but she doesn't work out with them.

Before a one-hour session gets underway, Al will tell his trainers if he is experiencing any aches or pains. When he was dealing with low-back pain, Melanie and April changed his routine to help him.

April said, "Clients should be vocal. Tell me when something hurts. He has my full attention. His back pain was better in three days."

She knows a key to Al's weight management is his ability to control his portions. He is disciplined.

April does cardio work on her own six days a week, and does weight training five or six days a week.

"Everybody should get thirty minutes of activity every day. Moving, stretching, getting into a pool. It doesn't count when people say I worked all day, and I was on my feet all day. You need to isolate and concentrate. You need to be in it physically. People who give excuses are only hurting themselves. You hurt yourself when you cheat. Most of the time they say they are too busy working, or are busy with their family. They are tired."

Al is April's oldest student. She is a big fan.

"He's a very kind, genuine, giving man, who has made a significant impact on a lot of people's lives. He knows a lot of people. A lot of people love him for good reason."

Melanie actually has a couple of clients who have been around longer than Al. One woman is eighty-eight, the other is eighty-nine.

April would like to see more seniors get as involved as Al Gray.

"Sometimes a broken hip, you don't recover. But when you have the support of all of your joints, tendons and ligaments, and you do fall, hopefully it's not the end of your mobility."

Melanie is dazzled by Al's steadfast determination.

"It's one of the most important things that he lives by. He shares with me how he sees so many of his contemporaries and friends who are not in good shape, and who are suffering from medical problems, or who have a tough time getting around. He is so vital, and has such an active life. It's so important to him. He doesn't see himself any other way. He wants to continue that. It's really what drives him. He doesn't need encouragement because he is so committed to doing it."

Melanie's dad David is impressed Al can stay so focused on business matters.

"He is extremely intelligent and bright. He might forget things momentarily, but he is very analytical and very thorough. Sometimes we have to repeat things or stay after him to find things or get things, but he always gets them. He picks people to surround himself with he feels he can trust. He will rely on them to make sure he's not missing anything. Al stays very involved. We often talk two or three times a week."

Thirty-four-year-old Geoff Hanks said, "Al is eighty-two years old this year, and he's more active than I am."

Stockbroker Scott Fisher says Al strives to stay fit every way he can.

"He's aware of his mortality. He's aware of what happens to people as life goes on. So he's got trainers to help him keep his body going. Investing in the stock market is the other half of the equation. It keeps his mind young and active."

Melanie said, "In all of the years I have known him, maybe twice he called and said he just couldn't do it because he had a horrible night's sleep and he just wasn't feeling well."

Al is good at multi-tasking. His hour workouts are a time for socializing as well.

Melanie said, "I look forward to it because we have such a great time. It almost doesn't seem like work to me. We catch up on how his family is doing. He tells me about things he has been doing. He tells me all of these stories. He's never at a loss for a story."

Don't Look Back

Walk into a law school today, and you will see a large number of women enrolled. That wasn't the case at the Western Reserve law school in 1945, right after the end of World War II. Al's class started out with 120 students. Only two were women.

One of Al's classmates was Ed Gold. They had been casual friends in their schoolboy days. Ed was a couple of years older than Al. During the time at Roxboro Junior High, Ed had served as sports editor of the Roxboro Rocket. Al would take on that task after Ed had graduated.

Ed said, "I think the only things we had in common were our joint interests in sports, the Indians and the Browns, and our social lives pursuing young women."

Al and Ed reconnected when they entered law school. Ed says sports and girls remained their connecting points.

"Al didn't enjoy speaking of academics because he wasn't interested in them. He's a bright gentleman. He was able to get by very easily. During those three years at law school, I recognized him as someone who was more interested in business than in law. I have a memory of him always following the Tokyo Stock Exchange. He was the only one saying you gotta go with the Japanese after World War II."

Al admits he was often razzed for bringing a Wall Street Journal to class with him every day.

While in law school, Al was already charting his course through the world financial markets.

Al was among the youngest students in his law school class. Many, like Ed, had served overseas in the war. They were given academic credits for their time in the military. When Ed Gold began his undergraduate studies at Western Reserve, he was ranked as a second-semester junior. Some of the beginning law students were twenty-five years old, or even older.

Ed said, "We were very serious. We wore suits or sport coats every day. We were older than what you might find today in law school. We were very attentive. Because of our service in the military, we knew how to take orders. You could hear a pin drop during a class session. There was no nonsense with this group."

Some members of the class would take a much-deserved break from academics by taking part in the law school's baseball team. Al talks about how he devoted much of his childhood to playing sandlot baseball. Ed wasn't convinced those years translated into ability on the Western Reserve Law School team.

"He was so enthusiastic about coming out for the team. We put him at second base, but I don't think he was an athlete. You never know until a guy got out onto the field. Alvin was a little disappointing at second base. He had a little problem with ground balls."

Ed was a pitcher on that team. He knows Al has achieved a lot in his life.

"I just don't need him as a second baseman. I can tell you that."

Al defends his diamond prowess.

"I was a little better hitter than fielder, but I wasn't so bad at either. I had learned how to bat both right-handed and left-handed. I had a lot of fun growing up with baseball. I wasn't so bad."

Ed was one the best students in that law class. He won numerous academic honors. He and Al would go on to become young lawyers in Cleveland.

Ed said, "He had a good reputation in practicing law. He was a perfect gentleman. He always had the best-looking receptionist in town."

Al worked hard, but always loved to live it up.

Ed said, "For his fortieth birthday, he got himself a bus and took us to some nice place and we had a ball. I was honored to be included. It was a night to remember. He knew how to party."

Ed knows Al likes to dress in a flashy manner and attract attention.

"Nine out of ten people would say that man dresses uniquely. Yet he feels good in his garb. He sees that as being stylish. He is seeing things obliquely, perhaps. I don't know what he is seeing through his eyes."

Ed was in his early sixties when he moved to Los Angeles. Al was determined not to lose touch with his law school buddy.

"Al's a master of trivia in sports. He would send me items cut out from the *Plain Dealer* which brought up some unique fact in the history of sports. I must have received fifty of those from him."

Ed enjoyed getting those sports clippings from Al. He had no idea that his good buddy was confronting demons. Al was slipping away. Ed returned to Cleveland for a law school reunion. He was stunned to see Al overcome with mental problems.

"I sat with him for a couple of hours and he was catatonic. I was shocked to find that was the case. I was terribly chagrined. It hurt me very much, because I remembered this was the guy I used to talk to about sports and women. He couldn't speak. I don't know who brought him to the reunion. It was such a shock to me and I felt for him so much. I was his pal, his buddy, and I was loyal to him."

Ed and his wife Elaine divorced. He said it was a peaceful parting. It was about the same time that Al's mental difficulties led to the end of his marriage with Anita. Al has now been able to develop a friendship with Anita, but Ed says Al's memory is a bit cloudy when it comes to the divorce.

"He always said to me his divorce ended amiably, but during the battle time it was bitter. I remember when they were going to war over a painting. Today, Al will say they got along just fine back then."

Ed is proud of his friend for putting his life back together. He respects all of Al's accomplishments.

"He had made substantial philanthropic donations to Jewish and scholastic causes and unequivocally, I would say I admire him. He puts his mark on things."

Ed knows Al loves to bask in the glow of recognition.

"I'm not saying it out of envy cause recognition is not important to me, however, it seems to be important to him. It's Al's story that attracts his center of attention. He was anxious to get into the Cleveland Heights High Hall of Fame. He was turned down the first time, so he hired a public relations person to put it together for him and he scored, he got it."

Ed was among those who attended Al's eightieth birthday party. The law school honored him by naming a section of the building after him.

Ed said, "I was happy for his happiness. He was in his element. He was so thrilled. I was happy to be in the presence of a guy who was seemingly on top of the world. More power to him."

Al is among the distinguished law school graduates who have been enshrined in an organization called the Society of Benchers.

Ed said, "I'm happy for him to be in the group."

Al is a different kind of guy in so many ways. When it comes to a sense of humor, he is not what one might call mainstream.

Ed summed it up by saying, "In his sense of humor, sometimes I didn't know he was trying to be funny. I don't mean to say this in bad faith, but there was often a good deal of sarcasm. Alvin really isn't funny in the sense of Seinfeld funny. He's sardonic. I consider myself as having a very good sense of humor. I'm referred to as really being funny. I couldn't make a living out of it, but he decries funny. He'll be totally exaggerative, thinking it's funny but it isn't. He's no Mark Twain."

Al's cousin David Kottler is less critical about Al's sense of humor.

David said, "On a scale of one to ten, I would give him a three on a sarcasm scale. He has a great sense of humor It's a little dry. I don't consider it sarcastic."

Ed classifies Al as one of his "character" friends. He doesn't mean that in a bad way.

"He's an interesting man. He is unique. Truly unique."

Ed knows that some people would look at Al Gray and think his personality has some rough edges. To some, he might come across as a difficult.

Ed jokes, "He's lucky to have me as a friend."

Being a friend of Al Gray's, takes some effort and a definite commitment. There is effort involved. Ed Gold is happy he has been able to nurture the relationship over all the decades. He knows Al's comments can be off-the-wall and misinterpreted from time to time. Al can be clever. His remarks are many times extremely funny, but his attempts at humor can sometimes fail miserably.

"It can be intolerable. It's not enjoyable. He doesn't mean it, but generally, some things he says could be considered a slight. He sees things differently. I don't think there are going to be a lot out there who say they love him. Well, I say that. I love him. Yes I'm going to say that."

Ed thinks Al shoots from the hip. The problem is, he can misfire.

"I could have become ignited by some of his responses, but it can be wise to think before you speak."

Ed has learned to brush off some of Al's comments. Just move on.

"That way, you are protecting the relationship. Someone has to. Al doesn't think about protecting the relationship."

Ed deeply values Al's friendship, even if it means giving him a free pass on what others might consider an unkind statement.

"He's a loyal friend and I hope to be described as a friend to him."

Ed Gold remains calm when talking to his friend Al. He has urged his children to take a reserved approach with people in their lives who could upset them. Just think before you speak.

"Most times, we act impulsively with people."

Ed has a long history with Al. He says their friendship has been meaningful.

"This guy means good. He has done good. He's an achiever. He's entitled to recognition. So let's put him up there. I have never angered him, taunted him, said anything that I would have taken back. I know where he is in the spectrum. I know where I placed him. He's probably planning a major escapade as we speak. I can just feel it."

Joel Fox remembers Al's welcomed involvement in a potentially dangerous situation at the Mayfield Road JCC in 1978. A community meeting was being held in Mandel Hall. Joel was in his early twenties. He was assigned to man a table outside the meeting room.

"I was alone in the lobby and approached by a young man from my back, and he had a knife which he held to my neck. I was able to talk him down and have him back off. He was a member of the Jewish community and had a chronic mental illness. He was very disturbed."

Al Gray intervened. Joel was naturally upset and didn't know what to do next. He said Al eased him through the trauma of that moment.

"Al was a lawyer and president of the JCC. He very lovingly and carefully guided me through that situation. We didn't press charges. Al joined me later when I met with the boy and his mother. She was desperate for there not to be any criminal charges against this very troubled young man. I remember Al, very lovingly talking to all of us in a way that was going to be most constructive for all parties. That was the beginning of my friendship with Al Gray."

Gary Simson said, "He's unique. He's interesting. He's fun. He's got a fabulous sense of humor. He's great to be around."

Al has never lost touch with the Case Western Reserve Law School. He is eager to provide monetary support and when there are events at the school he enjoys chatting with the current law students.

Gary Simson said, "He remembers it was a great place for him and he wants to make it as good for other people. You just value having people like Al."

Jim Bradlin has appreciated Al being a loyal customer at James Clothiers, but has also developed a deep appreciation for Al as a remarkable person.

"I think he's very intelligent. I think he has a way of communicating with people that brings you in, and you feel close to him without really knowing him. A lot of people don't expose their eccentricities. Al does. That's one of the reasons I like him so much. He's different. He calls a spade, a spade. You'll always get an honest answer from him."

Jim says whenever Al is in the store, there are customers he knows.

"He can talk to the busboy at the restaurant and the President of the United States. He is always socially involved."

David Kottler said, "Al's proud of his family heritage. The family is proud of him. I think he's exceptionally sincere. He's a humanitarian. I think he's full of life. I think most people would be eager to sign a contract to be where he is at age eighty-two, health-wise, career-wise, financially, philanthropically, and family-wise."

David said Al had the inner strength to overcome many obstacles. He dealt with the Great Depression in his early days.

"Anyone who grew up in that Depression era has learned a lot of life's lessons. They came up in a very difficult way. They came up very poor. Hard work was a big part of their work ethic. I don't think the kids today have the same work ethic."

David says after attaining many benchmarks of success in life, Al then had to confront mental illness.

David said, "You probably cannot recover from something like that until you are willing to go outside yourself and help other people. If you are going to dwell on what your problems are, or how you were wronged, then you will never recover. The key to his recovery was his willingness to help others."

Al's cousin Adam Fried said, "I think he just loves living. He doesn't look like he's eighty-two. He doesn't act like he's eighty-two. Those are not easy things to accomplish."

Geoff Hanks is amazed by the incredible pace Al maintains.

"He still works very hard. A lot of people are content to fulfill the persona of who they are and just sit back and let it work for itself.

He doesn't sit back. I think he has a sense of pride. He has never got out of touch with what it meant to bust your ass. No matter what he accomplished, he understood why he accomplished it. It still boils down to hard work and dedication. No matter what you are doing. He never has let that fall off and I have really taken that lesson from him."

Stephen Hoffman said, "Al is generous of spirit. He'll watch your back. He's a very loyal friend, and that's not a quality to be taken for granted."

Gerry Goldberg said, "Al wants people to like him. He's humorous. He's got self-confidence. He wants success, not just so he can have the trappings of success. He wants what you can do with success. He wants to make sure his family is financially independent and has no worries."

Gary Simson said, "I describe him as an incredibly upbeat person. Truly, I have never heard Al say anything negative about anybody. It's not like he doesn't see people the way they really are. I'm sure he sees flaws, but I think his feeling is he'd rather look for the good in people. Not dwell on the bad. He's an incredibly refreshing person."

Arlene Fine knows Al has touched a lot of lives. She said he has had a definite influence on her family.

"He's just a dear guy. He's a lot of fun. He's well-intended. He follows through with commitments. He's grounded our lives. He's added a lovely dimension. He's a character. He's a favorite uncle. I feel very grateful I sat next to him at that Ho Mita Koda fundraiser."

Al Gray has taken on the role of uncle to many, but he is the real uncle of Carol Marger. She says he has been a great one.

"He is very encouraging. If I am ever frustrated, or not sure how to handle something, he is always supportive. 'You are doing a good job. A great job. Keep it up.' That's nice. He's a positive voice out there. He likes to make a difference. He has great ideas. He has a lot of experience. He has a lot of different experiences and a lot of successes."

Arlene says her family members from Al's generation have died. Al fills a void.

"To have this nice man in our lives, is special. He always asks about our kids. That's nice. He's one of a kind."

Al has shared an important life lesson with Arlene.

"He used to say D.L.B. Don't look back. It's really good advice. What has happened, has happened. If you dwell on the past, and look back all the time, you can't look forward. I try to let go of things. I think that is part of the secret to his success."

Al said, "Don't look back suggests not dwelling on the past. You can observe it. You can reflect on it. Don't look back in a negative sense that it upsets you to look back. Some people spend their whole life crying about the past. I'm not a crier. Mental illness was a learning experience. I don't look back at the pain it caused me, and say boy, that was a terrible experience. I was there. You can look back, but don't let it overwhelm you. That's bad. It's good to look at the future because you can talk about optimistic viewpoints."

Arlene said, "He's excited for each day. A lot of older people gripe and complain about this and that. He's always going out. The phone doesn't stop ringing. People of all ages call him for lunch or for dinner. They invite him to parties. We should all have uncles like him. He would make life a lot more interesting."

Carol Marger said, "He's an honorable person. I feel fortunate Uncle Al has been in my life. He's shown me a lot of things I would have never seen. He has always had an intellectual curiosity. He reads a lot. He's passionate about things. He always got himself involved in one thing or another. He wants to be around to see his family grow up. He wants to help them shape their future."

Vi Spevack

Vi Spevack has written a gossip column for the *Cleveland Jewish News* called Cavalcade. She has been doing the column for forty-five years. That run is amazing in its own right, but when you consider she was forty-eight years old when she started doing it, makes it even more incredible.

If she had a nickel for every time she has seen Al Gray at a fundraiser or a community event, she would have amassed a nice chunk of change by now. They complement each other perfectly. Vi knows Al as well as anyone does.

"He actually wooed me as a friend, and I accepted it because he's the kind of guy I can call up and tell him something that's bothering me. I can scold him. I can confide in him, and I can commiserate with him. He's really my best girlfriend. I feel very close to him and I'm very honest with him. He does have a very good listening ear. He loves the company of women."

In referring to Al as a "girlfriend," Vi means no harm or disrespect. She is proud of the friendship she has developed with Al over the decades. They are comfortable with each other. There is no pretense.

"I can reveal my true self to him because I know he understands. He has a very compassionate heart. He's a very understanding person. His generosity supersedes everything. He has a generosity of spirit. He is a lover of people on many levels. He is very grateful to people who do even the smallest thing for him."

Violet Spevack has interviewed hundreds of people in her career. She has discovered that the most interesting people often have homes that are in total disorder. Al's home fits into that description.

"He never found a piece of paper, he didn't love. People like Al are just interested in so many things. Their homes reflect all of their interests."

Violet has developed a true respect for Al.

"He's a simple, yet complex man. He has lived his life very graciously after so many setbacks. He had a lot of disappointments and he just dealt with his life. He has emerged as a rather heroic figure. He is uniquely his own self. He doesn't change. I think he always wants to be who he is."

Violet knows that Al embraces his life. He can look back and take pride in his accomplishments, but is Al Gray a happy man?

"I don't know if he's happy. I don't know if he knows what happiness is. He seems to need friendships. He winds up being friends with the most unlikely people in the world. He never made a friend he doesn't keep forever. He cherishes friendships and he becomes a very loyal friend."

Violet says Al's sense of humor can sometimes be " a little quirky." She describes him as "a true original." She says there's no one quite like him.

"He has lived his life so valiantly. The collapse of his marriage was difficult for him, but life is what it is. Life is what we live."

Regrets and Hope for the Future

"If I had to do it all over again, there were a lot of things I would have changed. That's what a lifetime teaches you. My motto is: you want to be right 51% of the time.

"The first thing is, I would have wanted to control the dimensions of my illness to a greater degree than I was able to do, so that my marriage would not have ended, and my children, as well as Anita, wouldn't have been put through what they were.

"I wish I could have helped my dad to avert his terrible end. That had such an effect on my illness. It created the conditions from which my illness came.

"I know I have made huge mistakes, as we all do in our lifetimes. I have been able to minimize the effect of many of them, and as a result, I came out better than I might have on a lot of them."

Al says dealing with his father's gambling, and taking the blame for his disappearance, had a major impact on his life. The resulting mental breakdown was a heavy burden.

"There are lessons to be learned in life that you should reflect on, and I do. One of the values in living as long as I have, with a pretty clear mind, is that I have been able to think about things and not kick myself. Put things in the right perspective, so you can think things out pretty well.

"Maybe I didn't register things as completely as I might have. I didn't take time to think out as much as I might, and I didn't take all the facts into account. I am not chastising myself. I think it is important to learn the hard way."

Al likes to believe the second time a situation arises, he will be better prepared to deal with it. He doesn't want to make the same mistake twice.

"You are not going to do everything right, or perfectly. You do as much as you can, but realize, even with the best of attitude, the best of morality, you make huge mistakes and you have to manage them. You are very lucky if in a lifetime, you don't make a huge number of mistakes.

"Some people never seem to make right judgments at all, and their lives reflect it. I think I have been fortunate that people have been good to me, been thoughtful, kind and generous. I have taken advantage of opportunities.

"You have to enjoy what you do well. If you can do that, you are half-way home in career and opportunities. Too many people have to do what they have to do, instead of what they want to do. Work your butt off to get your best opportunities, and then convert those opportunities. Be prepared to admit mistakes. Be positive, but don't be smug. We all tend to get too cocky.

"The terrible time of my illness can't be underestimated. The impact it had on me and my family. I was thrashing around without success on my own. Finally, I admitted I ought to get some help. I was fortunate to be able to work through my problems and come out on the right end of it."

Al is aware a good number of people don't come back from the devastating setback he endured.

"I have great empathy for people. I try to give people advice on how to seek therapy and how to get help. The cost of treating mental illness is so high for so many people, it's extremely hard to get adequate therapeutic help. That's a terrible challenge for our society. We don't fully appreciate the number of people who need mental therapy. It's a huge number. We don't have enough money to work all those things through."

Al has enjoyed the fruits of life. He has dealt with challenges. He knows things are tough for so many.

"Day to day living in so many countries is loaded with danger. I would say our society has more pressure because of the complexities of society."

Lottie Gray has tremendous respect for her dad. He has remained strong through plenty of challenges.

"There's no possible way you can relate to growing up in that era, unless you grew up in that era. The Depression Era and World War II. It was such a different time. Anyone growing up in the world now couldn't understand the changes throughout the country and within the family back in those days. People who grew up in that era have a great appreciation for what they have been able to do for themselves."

Rachel says she has been touched by her dad's generosity, friendliness and compassion toward everyone.

"Strangers, everyone can be his best friend. His stubbornness is both good and bad. He has wisdom, practicality, and logic."

According to Anita, "He was always the smartest guy in the room. He's brilliant. He's a guy from humble beginnings. Many people may look at his story and find it sad and depressing. I don't look at it that way. I look at it as uplifting and a reaffirmation of life. We are all still chuggin' along. It's a beautiful story. It's a brilliant overcoming of the darkest of days that one person could possibly endure."

Al's advice about money.

"Get all you can honestly. Money is a means to lead a good life. I have had exciting opportunities. Part of that is luck, part is creative skill. I don't think I could consider at my age, what it would be like to live on Social Security. I don't think it is in the framework of my mind to live that way. I have lived much of my life in a better atmosphere than I started in."

Al says giving back is very important.

"You have to feel depressed about the people who have to live within limited means."

Al was asked why there are so many mean-spirited people in the world.

"It goes back to their youth. How they were raised, but perhaps that is an oversimplification. A large percentage of the population has mental problems, because the education system didn't get them on the straight track. The world is fast-moving, and many people are not able to keep up. They twist and turn in ways they shouldn't. People are looking for ways to punish others. They have no business doing that. People do dishonest things and then blame the system.

'Why did you steal, George?'

'Oh, that place is so crooked.'

"They think they are just trying to get back at someone. Some people choose to cheat on their spouses in a form of retaliation."

Al remains positive about people.

"I have the good fortune of enjoying the company of many people who made me feel better about life. Many people are not willing to open their minds and hearts to others, You've got to search around to find the good people. They don't just smile at you as you walk down the street."

LaVergne, TN USA
21 July 2010
190239LV00005B/1/P